Simon Peter

Simon Peter

by
Bruce E. Dana

BONNEVILLE BOOKS™

Springville, Utah

ISBN: 1-55517-701-8
e.2

Published by Bonneville Books
Imprint of Cedar Fort Inc.
www.cedarfort.com

Distributed by:

Typeset by Kristin Nelson
Cover design by Nicole D. Mortensen
Cover design © 2002 by Lyle Mortimer

Printed in the United States of America
10 9 8 7 6 5 4 3 2 1

Printed on acid-free paper

Library of Congress Cataloging-in-Publication Data

Dana, Bruce E.
  Simon Peter / by Bruce E. Dana.
    p. cm.
Includes bibliographical references and index.
  ISBN 1-55517-630-5 (pbk. : alk. paper)
  1. Peter, The Apostle, Saint. I. Title.
  BS2515 .D26 2002
  225.9'2--dc21

                    2002010066

Acknowledgments

Without the support of my wife, Brenda, this work would never have been written. Only those who write books, and especially doctrinal works, know of the tremendous amount of time spent in researching and writing them. Writers are born with a desire to write. I am grateful that my family allows me time to fulfill this desire.

I am thankful for all my children: Janalene, Connie, Michelle, Tami, Heather, Brooke, Benjamin, and Nathan; my parents, Edward and Shirley Dana, and my wife's parents, Max and Jody Lamb, for their constant love and devotion.

I am especially grateful for Lee Nelson and Lyle Mortimer of Cedar Fort, Inc., for their confidence in publishing my first two books, *Mysteries of the Kingdom* and *Mary, Mother of Jesus*. Truly, I express my appreciation to the staff of Cedar Fort—for their friendship and help in performing all of the necessary details that produce a professional and marketable product.

In writing this work, I am very grateful for my dear friend, Dennis "C" Davis, who, for thirty years, has generously shared his vast knowledge of the gospel with me. There are other trusted friends, Stephen Balls and Jean Britt, who have taken time to read my writings and given valuable comments and helpful suggestions.

I express my deepest respect for Elders Bruce R. McConkie and James E. Talmage, and the scholars, Alfred Edersheim and Frederic W. Farrar. The reader will gain a greater understanding of Simon Peter because of the inspired writings of these gifted authors.

In particular, I am thankful for Peter, the Rock and Seer. I pray that I have portrayed his life as accurately as possible.

Table of Contents

Preface

Among the Twelve Apostles chosen by our Lord, Peter's name appears most prominently. Regarding his character, the questions naturally arise: was he impulsive, reverent toward deity, or was he spiritually weak? From the scriptures and recognized scholars, this work will address these searching questions.

Peter was one of the greatest of all men. Due to the Bible being an abridgment of great and sacred events, only small glimpses of known facts are recorded of him. Silence is often prevalent in the scriptures concerning numerous personal matters. Notwithstanding, it is gratifying that we have been allowed to know what we do of the association and conversations between Jesus and his senior apostle.

In addition to more closely observing the social and personal characteristics of Simon Peter in the Jewish culture, it is most rewarding that we are allowed, to some degree, to understand his spiritual characteristics as well.

This work will not be a biography but more of a commentary and analysis of known events and actual conversations spoken and recorded in the New Testament. Due to the limited and abridged knowledge we have of Peter, a true biography cannot be written or even attempted. The reader should be aware that every commentary, including this work, contains a certain amount of opinion and speculation. No biography or commentary can totally avoid this.

Whenever a General Authority is quoted in this work, it is the right and responsibility of the reader to compare those quoted expressions with the scriptures found in the four

Standard Works of the Church, the words of the prophets, and official declarations issued by the First Presidency of The Church of Jesus Christ of Latter-day Saints. Then, through personal study and prayer, the reader can determine if the statements of the leading brethren are their own opinions or inspired words of truth.

From the New Testament, we discover how Simon's name was designated to be *Peter*. Andrew, who was Peter's brother, was converted to the teachings of John the Baptist. Later, Andrew and Peter traveled a great distance to meet the Messiah. Looking directly at Andrew's brother, our Lord spoke these revealing words: "Thou art Simon the son of Jona: thou shalt be called Cephas, which is by interpretation, A stone" (See John 1:42). From a *King James Version* Bible dictionary, we learn that his Aramaic name, *Cephas*, is the Greek equivalent of *Peter*.

Though there have been individuals who have pointed out the weakness of Peter, in various situations, it is important for the reader to remember that every person who is born on this earth, excepting our Lord, has weakness. This work will not emphasize Peter's weakness, but explain how his victory of overcoming them made him a great spiritual leader. With this introduction, let us discover what manner of man was chosen from among the hosts of heaven to become the senior, presiding apostle in Christ's church.

The reader is informed that various chapters in this book will contain the same information and wording as written in the author's book, *Mary, Mother of Jesus*. Both works contain information that pertains to, and give explanation about, Peter and his calling to be the senior apostle. The reader is further informed that the author has taken the liberty of correcting spelling errors and capitalization in some of the quoted text.

Introduction

In his scholarly book, *Jesus the Christ*, Elder James E. Talmage quotes from Alfred Edersheim, who, though not Jewish, was a recognized Jewish scholar, and Frederic W. Farrar, who was a Biblical scholar from the Church of England. Likewise, Elder Bruce R. McConkie, in his scholarly series *The Mortal Messiah: From Bethlehem to Calvary*, also quotes from these same authors. To help the reader understand why Elders Talmage and McConkie quote from these respected scholars, who wrote their works over one hundred years ago, I use the words penned by Elder McConkie: "At this point a word about almost all sectarian commentaries and biographies about Christ might not be amiss. It is my judgment that most of the modern publications are far from faith promoting. In most cases it is necessary to go back a hundred years or so to find authors who believed in the divine Sonship with sufficient fervor to accept the New Testament passages as meaning what they say . . ." (*The Mortal Messiah: From Bethlehem to Calvary*, Book 4, Note 2, p. 425) (Used by permission).

He further writes: "I have not hesitated to quote selected literary gems and to paraphrase others, . . . throughout this work, with particular reference to the writings of Edersheim and Farrar, two of the best sectarian authors . . ." (Ibid., Book 2, Note 2, p. 339) (Used by permission).

In addition, Elder McConkie writes these praising words about the book, *Jesus the Christ*: " . . . I have a deep and profound respect for *Jesus the Christ*, the scholarly work of

Elder James E. Talmage, one of my most prominent predecessors" (Ibid., Book 1, Preface, p. xvii).

In my judgment, other than the Prophet Joseph Smith, Elder Bruce R. McConkie is the premier doctrinal authority in the Church. His literary talents and doctrinal knowledge is well-known to the members of the Church. It is my prayer that all members of the Church will read and study the writings of this mighty apostolic witness of the Lord.

I am grateful to have the hundred-year-old books written by Edersheim and Farrar; further, to have the writings of Elders McConkie and Talmage. In writing my *Mary, Mother of Jesus* book and this work, *Simon Peter*, I quote frequently from the writings of these four recognized scholars. To explain why, I use the words written by Elder Bruce R. McConkie: "Short of receiving personal revelation on all points, no one author can think of all the meanings or set forth every nuance [awareness of meaning or value] of thought on all points. Further, it seems a waste of literary talent not to preserve some of the thoughts and modes of expression that those of old, who wrote on the same subjects, were led by the spirit of truth to record" (*The Mortal Messiah: From Bethlehem to Calvary*, Book 2, Note 2, p. 339) (Used by permission).

He then adds this interesting and insightful comment about quoting or paraphrasing the mentioned authors and not citing the reference: "Those who are acquainted with the original sources—be they [Edersheim or Farrar], or Josephus, Tacitus, or whosoever—will know that all authors have followed this practice. Elder Talmage does so in his scholarly work. It is also the course followed by the authors of the scriptures themselves, as when John the Apostle quotes and paraphrases, without identifying his original source, a prior account of John the Baptist, as is set forth in the first chapter of the Gospel of John" (Ibid., p. 339) (Used by permission).

The reader is informed that occasionally I, too, have followed this same practice. With this understanding, let us begin our study of the man called Simon Peter.

Chapter One

SIMON PETER WAS FOREORDAINED
(John 1: 42; Matt. 4: 18)

Prior to his earthly calling to be an apostle, Simon, who is better known as Peter, was foreordained to this high and holy office in the premortal existence. To support this declaration, the Prophet Joseph Smith (See Notes, end of chapter) revealed the following doctrine: "Every man who has a calling to minister to the inhabitants of the world was ordained to that very purpose in the Grand Council of heaven before this world was. [He then adds this insightful comment:] I suppose I was ordained to this very office in that Grand Council."[1]

Not only was Peter foreordained to become an apostolic witness of our Lord, he also was chosen to serve in the First Presidency of The Church of Jesus Christ. Later in this work, from the scriptures and the words of General Authorities, the reader will be given specific information to support this declaration. As it pertains to Peter, James, and John, Elder Bruce R. McConkie (See Notes 2, end of chapter) has written these declarative words: "Why were these three repeatedly singled out and given special blessings and privileges? . . . by latter-day revelation we know that they held and restored the keys of the kingdom, which belong always unto the Presidency of the High Priesthood (D&C 81: 2), or in other words, they were the First Presidency in their day."[2]

1

PETER WAS THE SENIOR APOSTLE
(Matt. 10: 2-4; Mark 3: 13-21; Luke 6: 12-16; Acts 1: 13-26)

Listing the names of the Twelve Apostles, who were called and ordained by our Lord, Matthew, Mark, and Luke place Peter's name first. From this information, we know that "Simon, who is called Peter," was the senior, presiding apostle. To further support this claim, we noticeably observe that throughout the New Testament, Peter's name always precedes those of James and John. Then, using the words of Elder James E. Talmage (See Notes 3, end of chapter), we read that after the death of Jesus, the "first official act undertaken by the apostles was the filling of the vacancy in the Council of the Twelve, occasioned by the apostasy and suicide of Judas Iscariot." [3] At a formal Church meeting, "*Peter* laid the matter before the assembled Church" and "affirmed the necessity of completing the apostolic quorum; and he thus set forth the qualifications essential in the one who should be ordained to the Holy Apostleship"[4] (italics added).

A "NOBLE AND GREAT" SPIRIT
(Abr. 3: 22-23; 2 Peter 1: 1)

By reason of his leadership role in the Church, we know that Peter was a "noble and great" spirit in the premortal life. To support this claim, we turn to Abraham's record and read his informative words: "Now the Lord had shown unto me, Abraham, the intelligences that were organized before the world was; and among all these there were many of the *noble and great ones*; And God saw these souls that they were good, and he stood in the midst of them, and he said: These I will make my rulers; for he stood among those that were spirits, and he saw that they were good; and he said unto me:

Abraham, thou art one of them; thou wast chosen before thou wast born" (italics added).

It needs to be emphasized that Simon Peter came into this world bringing with him the gifts and talents that he abundantly earned and developed in the premortal existence. He was prepared from before the foundation of this earth to become the senior member of the Twelve Apostles, who presided over Christ's Church, following the death of our Lord.

According to the terminology used in the time of Jesus, Peter was born into a Jewish family and not of a Gentile family. To understand the distinction, Elder Talmage explains: "In a general way the Jews designated all other peoples as Gentiles . . . the essential element of designation being that of foreigners . . . The injunction laid by Jesus upon the Twelve: 'Go not into the way of the Gentiles,' was to restrain them for the time being from attempting to make converts among the Romans and Greeks, and to confine their ministry to the people of Israel."[5] By reason of where he was born, Peter was raised in a Jewish family instead of a Gentile family. Therefore, he was honorably classified as a Jew.

NOTES

1. Joseph Smith, Jr. was the first President and prophet of The Church of Jesus Christ of Latter-day Saints. He received the Melchizedek Priesthood, and was ordained an apostle of Jesus Christ, in May 1829, by Peter, James, and John (See D&C 20: 2; 27: 12). Though he never served in the Quorum of the Twelve Apostles, the Prophet was the presiding apostle until his death.

At age 24, he was sustained as the First Elder of the Church on April 6, 1830; ordained a high priest on June 3, 1831; at age

26, he was sustained as President of the High Priesthood on January 25, 1832; at age 38, he was martyred at Carthage Jail, in Carthage, Illinois.

2. Elder Bruce R. McConkie was sustained to the First Council of the Seventy on October 6, 1946, at age 31; ordained an apostle, by President Harold B. Lee, on October 12, 1972, at age 57. He died April 19, 1985, at Salt Lake City, Utah, at age 69.

Elder McConkie was a prolific writer. He is recognized as one of the foremost gospel scholars in the Church. Part of his scholarly works include the following: *Mormon Doctrine*, The *Doctrinal New Testament Commentary* series, *The Mortal Messiah: From Bethlehem to Calvary* series; and, the last book written before his death, *A New Witness for the Articles of Faith*.

3. Elder James E. Talmage, ordained an apostle by President Joseph F. Smith, on December 8, 1911, at age 49. He died at Salt Lake City, Utah on July 27, 1933, at age 70. Among his scholarly works, he is most recognized for writing *Jesus the Christ*, a book that is endorsed and published by The Church of Jesus Christ of Latter-day Saints. He is also the author of *The Articles of Faith*.

Chapter Two

PETER WAS PLACED IN A JEWISH FAMILY

JEWISH AND GENTILE FAMILIES

To better understand why our Father in Heaven placed Peter—as he did Jesus and his mortal mother, Mary—in a Jewish family instead of a Gentile family, we turn to an eminent scholar, Dr. Alfred Edersheim (See Note 1, end of chapter) for information. Paraphrasing his words, we find that education began in the home for both the Jews and the Gentiles, and that the best homes were in Israel, because learning was imparted by influence and example before it came by teaching. We further discover what Jewish fathers and mothers were like, how they felt towards their children, and likewise how the children showed reverence and affection to their parents. Religious teachings truly influenced the child of Jewish parents.[6]

Edersheim mentions that it was no idle boast that the Jews were trained from birth to recognize God as their Father and as the Maker of the world; that they were taught the different laws, which were the laws of Moses and the laws of God. From their earliest youth, they learned these laws so that they became a part of their lives.[7]

He further stated that the Gentile world presented a terrible contrast from that of the Jewish world, especially regarding the relationship of parents and children and their character and moral upbringing.[8]

THE JEWS IN JESUS' DAY

In conjunction with Dr. Edersheim's comments, and with more clarification, we turn to a writing of Elder Bruce R. McConkie: "The law of family worship, the system revealed by the Great Jehovah to enable his people to gain exaltation through the continuation of the family unit in eternity, was known, in part at least, to the Jews in Jesus' day and in the true sense of the word to no other Old World people. Jewish families, therefore, had a religious foundation and a spiritual status totally unknown among the Gentiles . . . such families lived lives of decency and morality. Husbands and wives were faithful to each other, scriptural study and daily prayer were part of the rituals of life, and the family members lived honest, sober, and upright lives . . . .

"In contrast, family life among the Gentiles was defiled, corrupt, devoid of decency, and of such a low order as scarcely to be worthy of the name . . . ."[9]

Quoting from another of Edersheim's books,[10] Elder McConkie provides this information: "Strange as it may sound," Edersheim says, "it is strictly true that, beyond the boundaries of Israel, it would be scarcely possible to speak with any propriety of family life, or even the family, as we understand these terms . . . ."[11]

As it pertains to the Jews as a whole nation, Elder McConkie gives this explanation: "True, their knowledge was incomplete, and the full glory of perfect familial relationships had been lost among them. But they had been born in the family of Israel; the traditions of their fathers still lingered in their homes; and they did have the holy scriptures, wherein the Abrahamic covenant and the chosen status of Israel were extolled. They were, indeed, a unique people, a peculiar people, a people set apart from all others. Their family-centered way of life, their religious traditions, their social customs all combined to separate them, to make them a people without peer. . . ."[12]

Concerning our Lord, Elder McConkie wrote: "As we view Jewish families and Gentile families, is it any wonder that the Son of God came among the Jews? Though they would take his life in due course, because of priestcraft and iniquity, yet divine providence required an environment and a social and religious climate that would enable him to grow to maturity, unstained, preserved physically and spiritually, so that he could do his appointed work before he laid down his life as our Savior and Redeemer."[13]

PETER'S APPOINTED WORK

In conjunction with what Elder McConkie has written of our Savior, we know that Peter was also required to be raised in the same "environment." He was raised in a Jewish family so that he could do his "appointed work." His rewarding yet challenging work was to serve as the senior, presiding apostle.

NOTES

1. Alfred Edersheim was a scholar, holding three higher educational degrees, M.A., D.D., PH. D. He was an author over one hundred years past, who accepted Jesus Christ as the literal Son of God.

In *The Mortal Messiah* series, Elder McConkie has periodically quoted Edersheim. In addition, Elder McConkie has written praising words of this religious man. See Book 1, pp. 130-131, and Book 4, p. 425. note 3.

Chapter Three

PETER'S EDUCATIONAL PROCESS

THE PARENT'S ROLE

Being a unique people, Jewish parents taught and educated their children in Jewish practices as well as in the Law of Moses; first by example, then by instruction. To assist us in understanding how Peter, and other Jewish children were educated, we will use the pattern as outlined by Dr. Edersheim:

JEWISH MOTHERS

"The first education was necessarily the mother's."[14] In speaking of mothers, most will agree that this singular person's influence and instruction will leave a lasting impression upon a child. Whether for good or bad, a mother's example and instruction can influence the thoughts of every child. It is true that every child is born with its own unique personality and temperament; however, while still young and impressionable, it is the mother who can influence her child to become better or worse. As it pertains to Peter, we can assume that in addition to his premortal status as a "noble and great" spirit, he had a loving and caring mother who helped him to become the best that he could be.

Writing of the duties of a typical Jewish mother, our scholar explains:

"Other religious duties devolved exclusively upon them,

9

such as the Sabbath meal, the lighting of the Sabbath lamp, and setting the bread for the household . . . ."[15]

Even in our modern day, wherein many men are doing more domestic chores in the home, it is generally women who are the homemakers. Back in Jesus' day, and especially on the Sabbath, the homemaking duties were exclusively the mother's responsibility.

Continuing again with the role of a Jewish mother in educating her child, we learn this information: "Even before he [the child] could follow her in such religious household duties, his eyes must have been attracted by the Mezuzah attached to the doorpost . . . ."[16]

The Mezuzah was a little folded parchment, and on this parchment was the name of the Most High God; and was reverently touched by those who came or went into the home. In popular opinion it was the symbol of the divine guard over Israel's homes. Placing the Mezuzah near the front door of the home, with the name of the Most High God on it, was the responsibility of women.[17]

From his infancy, Peter observed his mother performing the mentioned household duties and responsibilities. Then, when Peter married, his wife performed these same domestic chores.

JEWISH FATHERS

We gather the following information about Jewish fathers. Again, paraphrasing the words of Edersheim:

It was the father who was bound to teach his son the knowledge of the Torah.[18] When the child learned to speak, his religious instruction was to begin with verses of Holy Scripture, short prayers, and select sayings of the sages.[19] Very early the child must have been taught some verse of scripture beginning with, ending with, or at least containing, the same letters as his Hebrew name. The earliest hymns taught would be the Psalms.[20]

In Jewish homes, the Law of Moses was taught and observed by all. From what has been written by Dr. Edersheim and Elder McConkie, Peter was taught and educated by the same parental process.

Chapter Four

FORMAL INSTRUCTION AND SCHOOLING
(Gen. 49: 10; JST Gen. 50: 24; John 1: 40-42)

Concerning the formal education of Jewish children, which included Peter, we rely once again upon Edersheim for information: "The regular instruction commenced with the fifth or sixth year, when every child was sent to school. There can be no reasonable doubt that at that time such schools existed throughout the land . . . ." Later in this same chapter, he further wrote, "Suffice it that, from the teaching of the alphabet or of writing, onwards to the farthest limit of instruction in the most advanced Academies of the Rabbis, all is marked by extreme care, wisdom, accuracy, and a moral and religious purpose as the ultimate object."[21]

As it relates to the respective studies according to age, we gain this knowledge: "Roughly classifying the subjects of study, it was held, that, up to ten years of age, the Bible exclusively should be the text-book (See Notes 1 and 2, end of chapter); from ten to fifteen the Mishnah, or traditional law; after that age, the student should enter on those theological discussions which occupied time and attention in the higher Academies of the Rabbis. Not that this progression would always be made."[22]

In conclusion, Edersheim has written these words of truth: "The teaching in school would, of course, be greatly aided by the services of the Synagogue, and the deeper influences of home-life."[23]

DELIVERER

From this information, three things can be concluded: First, these unique people began their formal schooling at age five or six, and completed it in their fifteenth year. Advanced studies were available, but not mandatory. Secondly, their studies were more of a religious nature than a secular one. As Edersheim has explained, "a moral and religious purpose was the ultimate object of the schools." Thirdly, though not mentioned by Edersheim, we know that both from their instruction in school, and the Bible, the Jews knew of the prophecies of the Promised Messiah, and looked forward for a Deliverer to "free them from personal and national bondage." On this subject, Elder McConkie has written these informative words: "It comes, therefore, as no surprise to find that all Israel in the days of Jesus were looking for a temporal Deliverer, for a Messiah born in the lineage of Abraham and David, who, sitting on the throne of their greatest king, would free them from personal and national bondage and vanquish their enemies. They looked for a preeminent Judahite ruler—for the scepter was not to depart from David's Judah until Shiloh [who is Christ] came—who would throw off the Roman yoke and scatter the legions of the Caesars . . . .

"Such a Deliverer, such a Messiah, as they envisioned, would not only restore the kingdom to Israel, but would also return the dispersed of that great nation to their original inheritance in their promised Canaan."[24]

From his religious training in the home and in the classroom, Simon Peter knew of and prayed for the fulfillment of the "Deliverer" when Andrew, his brother, brought him to meet the Messiah.

PETER GREW IN WISDOM AND STATURE
(Acts 4: 1-13)

When Peter and John, who then were in the First Presidency of the Church, were arrested because "they taught the people, and preached through Jesus the resurrection from the dead," the council asked the apostles: "By what power, or by what name, have ye done this?" After the apostles answered their question, we learn of the surprise of the leaders: "Now when they saw the boldness of Peter and John, and perceived that they were unlearned and ignorant men [meaning: ordinary or plain], they marvelled . . . ."

Because Peter and John had not gone to school in the "advanced Academies of the Rabbis," the council classified them as "unlearned." Having been taught by Jesus, the Master Teacher, they were wiser than the Rabbis.

Therefore, with a combination of his premortal nature, as well as the parental teachings in his Jewish home, and those in the formal Jewish school, Peter was specifically being brought up to become the presiding apostle in Christ's Church. From infancy to adulthood, Peter grew in wisdom and stature, both physically and spiritually.

NOTES

1. Dr. Edersheim has written what a student was taught in school:

"The study of the Bible commenced with that of the Book of Leviticus. Thence it passed to the other parts of the Pentateuch; then to the Prophets; and, finally, to the Hagiographa. What now constitutes the Gemara or Talmud was taught in the Academies, to which access could not be gained till after the age of fifteen. Care was taken not to send a child too early to school, nor to overwork him when there. For this purpose the school-hours were fixed, and attendance shortened during the summer months" (Edersheim 1: 232).

2. The parts of the Bible that were studied are as follows: Pentateuch is known as the first five books of the Old Testament. The Prophets are known as historical books like Joshua, Judges, 1, 2 Samuel, and 1, 2 Kings. The Hagiographa consists of the third of the three ancient Jewish divisions of the Old Testament, containing those books not in the Law (Torah) or the Prophets and usually include the Psalms, Proverbs, Job, the Song of Solomon, Ruth, Lamentations, Ecclesiastes, Esther, Daniel, Ezra, Nehemiah, and Chronicles. The Gemara is the second part of the Talmud, consisting chiefly of commentary of the Mishnah. The Mishnah is the first section of the Talmud, a compilation of early oral interpretations of the scriptures dating from about 200 A.D.

Chapter Five

PETER'S IMMEDIATE FAMILY
(John 1: 40-42; 6: 8; 21: 15-17; Matt. 4: 18; 10: 2; Mark 1:16; Luke 6:14)

Due to the New Testament being an abridgment of sacred writings, we do not know the number of individuals in Peter's immediate family. However, in the beginning of John's gospel, we find out that the name of Peter's father was "Jona." Then, later in his gospel, John wrote that his name was "Jonas." With this information, it is reasonable to believe that Jona was an abbreviated name for Jonas, and certain individuals, from time to time, called Peter's father by both names.

Matthew, Mark, Luke, and John have written that Andrew was Peter's brother. Judging from what they wrote, it is safe to believe that Andrew was Peter's only brother. However, these gospel writers do not tell which brother was the oldest, if they had a sister, or the name of their mother.

A BRIEF DESCRIPTION OF SIMON PETER

Regarding the Twelve Apostles chosen by our Lord, the scholars, Frederic W. Farrar (See Note 2, end of chapter), Alfred Edersheim, and the apostolic scholars, Elders Bruce R. McConkie, and James E. Talmage, have written a brief description of their individual lives (See Note 1, end of chapter). As it pertains to Simon Peter, we quote only a portion of what Elder McConkie wrote:

17

"This noble soul—chief of the apostles, valiant, courageous, conforming; as rugged and forceful as Elijah, who called down fire from heaven, and slew the priests of Baal with the sword; as submissive and spiritual as Samuel, who attuned his ear to hear the voice of God—Simon Peter was called by Jesus to preside over the earthly kingdom, to lay the foundation and build up that church which alone would administer salvation for that day and dispensation.

"We shall see him in many settings: forsaking all to follow Jesus; testifying of his divine Sonship in the coast of Caesarea Philippi: severing the ear of Malchus with a sword in Gethsemane; denying that he knows who Christ is in the courtyard of Caiaphas, the high priest; accusing the Jews, to their face, of murdering the Lord; penning the most sublime language in the New Testament; being crucified, head downward, for the testimony of Jesus that was his; coming in resurrected glory in 1829 to restore priesthood and keys and call men again to the holy apostleship."[25]

A BRIEF DESCRIPTION OF ANDREW

Turning our attention to Peter's brother, Elder Talmage says: "*Andrew*, son of Jona and brother of Simon Peter, is mentioned less frequently . . . . He shared with Peter in the honor of the call of the Lord on the sea shore, and in the promise 'I will make you fishers of men' . . . [See Matt. 4: 19]. Tradition is rife with stories about this man, but of the extent of his ministry, the duration of his life, and the circumstances of his death, we have no authentic record"[26] (italics in quotation).

SIMON PETER AND ANDREW

Therefore, as it relates to Simon Peter and Andrew, our Father in Heaven placed each of these noble and great men— just as he did Jesus—in a Jewish home, in order to prepare each to grow to maturity, unstained, preserved physically and spiritually, in order that individually and collectively they could do their appointed work. Peter's work was to be the senior, presiding apostle in Christ's church. Andrew's work was also to be an apostle, who served as a special witness of our Lord and Savior.

OTHER DISCIPLES

In order to understand how Peter became the chief apostle, we need to know that his brother was the person who taught him the gospel and brought him to meet the Messiah. After these brothers were called by our Lord to be disciples, they traveled with other disciples who were also called by Jesus. By reason that these disciples closely associated with Simon Peter, this work will briefly present information regarding their individual calls.

NOTES

1. Alfred Edersheim, *The Life and Times of Jesus the Messiah*, Book 1, pp. 521-523; Frederic W. Farrar, *The Life of Christ*, pp. 134-138; Elder Bruce R. McConkie, *The Mortal Messiah: From Bethlehem to Calvary*, Book 2, pp. 105-111; James E. Talmage, *Jesus the Christ*, pp. 218-226.

2. Frederic W. Farrar, an eminent scholar of the Church of England, with the titles of D.D. and F.R.S., was an author, over a hundred years past, who is noted for his literary talents and knowledge of the scriptures.

Elder Bruce R. McConkie, in his series, *The Mortal Messiah: From Bethlehem to Calvary*, has quoted frequently from the writings of Mr. Farrar. In addition, he has written praising words of this talented man—See book 4, pp. 180-191; page 425, Note 2.

Chapter Six

TRADE OF SIMON PETER AND ANDREW
(Matt. 4: 18-22; 14:13-23; 15: 32-39; Mark 1: 16-20; 6: 30-46; 8: 1-10; Luke 5: 7, 10; 24: 42-43)

From Matthew and Mark, we learn that Peter and Andrew were "fishers." Back in the time of Jesus—just as it is in our day—an honorable and needed vocation was commercial fishing. Fish not only supply food for people, but those people who buy fish supply a living for commercial fishermen. Such was the case with Simon Peter and Andrew.

To realize how important fish was in the diet of the Jews in the days of Jesus, Dr. Edersheim explains: "And as fish was among the favorite articles of diet, in health and sickness, on week-days and especially at the Sabbath-meal, many must have been employed in connection with this trade . . . . They were eaten fresh, dried, or pickled; a kind of 'relish' or sauce was made of them . . . ."[27]

Then, we remember that when Jesus fed four thousand people, the disciples had seven loaves of bread and "a few little fishes." Likewise, when he fed five thousand people, the disciples had fives loaves of bread and "two fishes." In addition, after Jesus was resurrected, he appeared to eleven of the apostles, "And they gave him a piece of a broiled fish, and of an [sic] honeycomb. And he took it, and did eat before them."

Turning our attention to the fishers, Simon Peter and Andrew, the Apostle Luke, in verse ten, states that the brothers, James and John "were partners with Simon." However, in verse seven, he says, "And they [Peter and Andrew] beckoned unto their partners, [James and John] which were in the other ship." To support that each set of brothers were partners, Elder Talmage has written: "He [Peter] and his brother Andrew were partners with James and John, the sons of Zebedee . . . ."[28]

With this understanding, let us turn our attention to a vocation in the time of Jesus. We begin by considering the trade of Joseph and Jesus.

A VOCATION IN THE TIME OF JESUS
(Matt. 13: 55; Mark 6: 3)

How was it that Joseph and Jesus were carpenters? Likewise, how was it that the brothers, Simon Peter and Andrew, and the brothers, James and John, were fishermen? To help find the answer, we again rely upon Elder Talmage for information:

"At twelve years of age a Jewish boy was recognized as a member of his home community; he was required then to enter with definite purpose upon his chosen vocation . . . ."[29]

With this knowledge, let us find out more of the trade of Simon and Andrew, and the brothers, James and John. Further, let us learn where Simon and Andrew were born and raised.

PETER AND ANDREW IN BETHSAIDA
(John 1: 44; Matt. 4: 18-21; Mark 1: 16-20; Luke 5: 1-11)

From John only, we discover that Peter, Andrew, and Philip—all of whom were future disciples and apostles of Jesus—were from the city of Bethsaida. It is worth noting that there were two cities known by this name. The following information is paraphrased from a Bible dictionary: Bethsaida was also known as the "house of fish" or "house of fishers." The older city was located on the west side of the Sea of Galilee, close to Capernaum, and was the home of Peter, Andrew, and Philip (John 1: 44; 12: 21). Philip the Tetrarch built a city that he called Bethsaida-Julias. The rebuilt city was north of the older town and probably was near the place where Jesus fed the five thousand (Mark 6: 45; Luke 9: 10) and healed a blind man (Mark 8: 22). When our Lord condemned Bethsaida for its unbelief (Matt. 11: 21; Luke 10: 13), he probably was referring to Philip's capital, not the older city where many fishermen lived.[30] By living in a city composed largely of fishermen, it would seem natural for Peter and Andrew to choose the trade of their father, Jona.

With reference to the father of James and John, Matthew, Mark, and Luke have written that Zebedee was a fisher. However, he was no common fisherman, for as Mark explains, he had "hired servants." Therefore, Zebedee was not poor, but wealthy. As was the custom of the day, he taught his sons, James and John, a valuable and profitable trade.

To support the theory that Zebedee was wealthy, Edersheim says: "They [the gospel writers] give a more vivid idea of life by the Lake of Galilee, and show that those engaged in that trade, like Zebedee and his sons, were not unfrequently [sic] men of means and standing."[31]

By reason that James and John were partners with Peter and Andrew, it would appear evident that they were "well-to-do" financially. Specifically speaking of Peter, Elder Talmage has written these declarative words: "He was well to do in a material way; and when he once spoke of having left all to follow Jesus, the Lord did not deny that Peter's sacrifice of temporal possessions was as great as had been implied"[32] (See Chapter Twenty-Seven in this work).

HOW AND WHEN THE BROTHERS MET

Due to the limited amount of knowledge that is written in the gospels, we do not know if Jona and Zebedee knew one another. Further, we are left without knowledge of when or how Peter and Andrew became acquainted with James and John, or when they agreed to be fishing partners. Because they were partners, we can safely believe that two factors caused this association: First, by being fishermen on the Sea of Galilee, their mutual trade enhanced the process of meeting one another. Secondly, because Peter and Andrew and James and John were called by our Lord to be apostles, we can conclude that divine providence caused them to join as partners, in order that they would closely know of the goodness and quality of each brother. Then, when Peter, James, and John served in the First Presidency, they were associated together in a holy partnership.

Chapter Seven

JAMES AND JOHN, FISHING PARTNERS WITH PETER

COLLECTIVELY CONSIDERED
(John 19: 25; Matt. 27: 56; Mark 15: 40)

To help us better understand who James and John were, Elder Talmage has written this description: *"James* and *John,* brothers by birth, partners in business as fishermen, brethren in the ministry, were associated together and with Peter in the apostolic calling. The Lord bestowed upon the pair a title in common—Boanerges, or Sons of Thunder—possibly with reference to the zeal they developed in His service, which, indeed, at times had to be restrained, as when they would have had fire called from heaven to destroy the Samaritan villagers who had refused hospitality to the Master. They and their mother aspired to the highest honors of the kingdom, and asked that the two be given places, one on the right the other on the left of Christ in His glory. This ambition was gently reproved by the Lord, and the request gave offense to the other apostles. With Peter these two brothers were witnesses of many of the most important incidents in the life of Jesus; . . ."[33] (italics included in quotation).

It is important to point out that in addition to being fishing partners with Peter and Andrew and serving together in the holy apostleship, James and John were also related to our Lord. Concerning this relationship, we turn our attention to the woman known as Mary, the mother of Jesus.[34]

MARY'S IMMEDIATE FAMILY

With the limited amount of knowledge that is revealed, we are not informed of the number of individuals in Mary's immediate family. However, by a careful reading of one scripture, found in the Gospel of John, we discover that this Jewish maiden had at least one sister:

"Now there stood by the cross of Jesus his mother, *and his mother's sister*, Mary the wife of Cleophas, and Mary Magdalene" (italics added) (John 19:25).

Regarding this scripture, Elder Talmage has written these informative words: "From the fact that John mentions the mother of Jesus and 'his mother's sister' (See John 19: 25) and omits mention of Salome by name, some expositors [those individuals who expound or explain] hold that Salome was the sister of Mary the mother of Jesus; and therefore the Savior's aunt. This relationship would make James and John cousins to Jesus. While the scriptural record does not disprove this alleged kinship, it certainly does not affirm the same."[35]

SALOME, THE SISTER OF MARY

Let us consider another point of view. Analyzing two New Testament scriptures, which speak of the mother of Zebedee's children, and the women called Salome, the reader can formulate who was the mother of James and John: "Among which was Mary Magdalene, and Mary the mother of James and Joses, and *the mother of Zebedee's children*" (italics added) (Matt. 27:56).

"There were also women looking on afar off: among whom was Mary Magdalene, and Mary the mother of James the less and of Joses, and *Salome*; (italics added) (Mark 15:40).

As it pertains to Mary and her sister, Dr. Edersheim has written these declarative words: "Thus Salome, the wife of Zebedee and St. John's mother, was the sister of the Virgin, and the beloved disciple the cousin (on the mother's side) of Jesus, and the nephew of the Virgin. This also helps to explain why the care of the Mother had been entrusted to him."[36]

In harmony with Edersheim's statement, Elder McConkie assuredly and without reservation has written: "Jesus' attention is now turned to a scene of sorrow and despair. By the cross stands his mother . . . . With her are three other faithful women—her sister, Salome, the wife of Zebedee and the mother of James and John (who thus were cousins of Jesus), Mary the wife of Cleophas; and Mary Magdalene."[37]

REGARDING JAMES AND JOHN

Therefore, as it relates to Mary and her sister, Salome, our loving Father in Heaven placed each of these noble and great ladies—just as he did Jesus and Peter—in a Jewish home, in order to prepare each to grow to maturity, unstained, preserved physically and spiritually, in order that individually and collectively they could do their appointed work. Mary's work was to be the mother of Jesus. Salome's work was to be the mother of James and John, who in turn became apostolic witnesses of their first cousin and Lord. In addition to becoming apostolic witnesses of their first cousin, they also served as counselors in the First Presidency with Simon Peter as the President of the Church, following the death of Jesus.

Chapter Eight

ANDREW AND JOHN FOLLOWED JESUS
(Matt. 3: 13-17; 10: 2-4; 4: 1-11; JST Matt. 4: 1-2; Mark 1: 9-
13; 3: 13-21; Luke 3: 21-22; 4: 1-14; 6: 12-16; John 1: 28; 1 Ne.
1: 10-11;11: 29, 34-36; 12: 9)

JESUS BEGAN HIS MINISTRY

Preparatory to understanding how Peter became a disciple
of our Lord, we must first learn how his brother, Andrew, and
their mutual fishing partner, John, became disciples of Jesus.
It is important to know that Andrew's conversion led to the
conversion of Peter.

The day finally arrived that Jesus began his formal
ministry. Following the baptism of Jesus by John the Baptist,
"in Bethabara beyond Jordan," he "was led up of the Spirit, into
the wilderness, to be with God." Then, after he "had communed
with God, he was afterwards an hungered, and was left to be
tempted of the devil." Triumphantly resisting the temptations
of Satan, we learn that "Jesus returned in the power of the
Spirit into Galilee." Beginning his ministry, our Lord donated
all of his time and talents to teaching his fellowmen the saving
truths of his glorious gospel.

Part of Jesus' communion with his Father was to know the
disciples who would serve with him in his early ministry.
Following his forty days of fasting, our Lord knew who they
were. Two of these twelve men were disciples of John the
Baptist.

TWO DISCIPLES OF JOHN THE BAPTIST
(John 1: 29, 35-40)

The day after Jesus was baptized, John the Baptist saw "Jesus coming unto him." With conviction, John the Baptist spoke these revealing words to all the people who were gathered together, "Behold the Lamb of God, which taketh away the sin of the world."

Specifically referring to Peter's brother, Andrew, and an unnamed disciple, Farrar explains: "But on the second day, when [John] the Baptist was standing accompanied by two of his disciples, Jesus again walked by, and John, fixing upon Him his intense and earnest gaze, exclaimed again, as though with involuntary awe and admiration, 'Behold the Lamb of God!'"[38]

For reasons of his own, Jesus did not stop and talk to John, or "two of his disciples," but continued on his way. Relying again upon Farrar, we read what transpired next: "The words were too remarkable to be again neglected, and the two Galilean youths who heard them followed the retreating figure of Jesus. He caught the sound of their timid footsteps, and turning round to look at them as they came near, He gently asked, 'What seek ye?'"[39]

Whether both disciples spoke in unison, or only one was the spokesman, we read, "They said unto him, Rabbi, (which is to say, being interpreted, *Master*) where dwellest thou?"

Courteously, our Lord replied, "Come and see." Whether it was out of curiosity, or with a real desire to know, the two disciples "came and saw where he dwelt, and abode with him that day: for it was about the tenth hour."

As to where Jesus was staying, Farrar has honestly written: "Where it was we do not know. Perhaps in one of the temporary *succoth*, or booth, covered at the top with the striped *abba*, which is in the East an article of ordinary wear, and with their

30

wattled sides interwoven with green branches or terebinth or palm, which must have given the only shelter possible to the hundreds who had flocked to John's baptism"[40] (italics in quotation).

With reference to the wording, "for it was about the tenth hour," and the time that the disciples spent with our Lord, Farrar explains: "They came and saw where Jesus dwelt, and as it was then four in the afternoon, stayed there that day, and probably slept there that night; and before they lay down to sleep they knew and felt in their inmost hearts that the kingdom of heaven had come, that the hopes of long centuries were now fulfilled, that they had been in the presence of Him who was the desire of all nations, the Priest greater than Aaron, the prophet greater than Moses, the King greater than David, the true Star of Jacob and Scepter of Israel."[41]

With another view, Edersheim states: "It was but early morning—ten o'clock."[42] To clarify, he wrote: "The common supposition is, that the time must be computed according to the Jewish method, in which case the tenth hour would represent 4 P.M. But remembering that the Jewish day ended with sunset, it could, in that case, have been scarcely marked, that 'they abode with Him that day.' The correct interpretation would therefore point in this, as in other passages of St. John, to the Asiatic numeration of hours, corresponding to our own . . . ."[43]

Whether it was "ten o'clock" in the morning or "four in the afternoon," these new disciples were blessed to spend quality time with our Lord. Whatever was spoken in this special setting, we know these disciples gained a strong testimony that Jesus was the Messiah.

In a future day, Andrew and John, along with their brothers, Peter and James, would spend more than a day and a night with Jesus. All of them would spend thousands of hours with our Lord.

JOHN, THE UNNAMED DISCIPLE

With reference to Peter's brother and the unnamed disciple, Farrar has written these informative words: "One of those two youths who thus came earliest to Christ was Andrew. The other suppressed his own name because he was the narrator, the beloved disciple, the Evangelist St. John. No wonder that the smallest details, down even to the very hour of the day, were treasured in his memory, never to be forgotten, even in extreme old age."[44]

ANDREW DESIRED TO TELL SIMON PETER
(See John 1: 28, 41-42)

After spending glorious time with Jesus, Andrew now does what every new convert should do—he desired to share the savings truths of the gospel with members of his family. Accordingly, Andrew was anxious to find his brother, Simon Peter. (Likewise, we may properly believe that John was anxious to find his brother, James.) To demonstrate his resolve, it is reasonable to believe that Andrew traveled a distance of approximately sixty miles to tell his brother, who was probably still living in Bethsaida. When Andrew finally found Peter, he declared with excitement and conviction, "We have found the Messias, [sic] which is, being interpreted, the Christ."

We are not informed of all that was spoken between these brothers, but we can imagine that the Spirit guided Andrew's words. Further, that the Spirit bore witness to Peter of the truthfulness of his brother's testimony.

Exhibiting a trait that would exemplify his life in the ministry of our Lord, Peter "believed" the words of Andrew. Accordingly, these noble brothers traveled approximately sixty miles to Bethabara, whose exact location is not known, but tradition places it near the city of Jericho.[45]

Chapter Nine

THE MEANING OF PETER'S NEW NAME

"BELIEVING BLOOD"

It is natural to ask the following questions: Why did Andrew and John look for John the Baptist? What caused Andrew and John to become disciples of Jesus? Likewise, what caused Peter to believe the words of his brother, Andrew, and travel a great distance to meet the Messiah?

To help answer these questions, we use the words of Elder McConkie: "Why is it easy for some people to believe in Christ, in his prophets, and in his gospel? Why do others reject the gospel, persecute the prophets, and even deny the divinity of Him whose gospel it is? . . .

"To this problem there is no easy answer. Every person stands alone in choosing his beliefs and electing the course he will pursue . . . . But in the final sense the answer stems back to premortality. We all lived as spirit beings, as children of the Eternal Father, for an infinitely long period of time in the premortal existence . . . .

"And as it is with the prophets, so is it with all the chosen seed. 'God's elect,' as Paul calls them (Romans 8: 33), are especially endowed at birth with spiritual talents. It is easier for them to believe the gospel than it is for the generality of mankind."[46]

Elder McConkie goes on to explain that "the noble and great ones" are sent to earth in "favored families."[47] Concerning

33

the doctrine of "believing blood," our apostolic scholar asks and answers this intriguing question: "What then is believing blood? It is the blood that flows in the veins of those who are the literal seed of Abraham—not that the blood itself believes, but that those born in that lineage have both the right and a special spiritual capacity to recognize, receive and believe the truth . . . . It identifies those who developed in preexistence the talent to recognize the truth and to desire righteousness."[48]

From this inspired explanation, we know why Andrew and John, and their individual brothers, Peter and James, readily recognized and believed the truth. With this realization, let us find out what happened when Peter met the Savior.

"THOU SHALT BE CALLED CEPHAS"
(John 1: 42)

Visualize Andrew and Peter walking side by side toward our Lord. When they met Jesus, Andrew, with courtesy and respect, introduced his brother. It is reasonable to believe that several minutes of pleasant conversation were exchanged between our Savior and these two brothers. With each word spoken by the Son of God, Peter gained a burning testimony that Jesus was the Christ. Using the well-chosen words of Edersheim, we read what transpired next: "The searching, penetrating glance of the Saviour now read in Peter's inmost character his future call and work . . . ."[49] Then, from the scriptural record, we read these powerful and meaningful words regarding one of the greatest of all men: "Thou art Simon the son of Jona: thou shalt be called *Cephas*, which is by interpretation, *A Stone*."

Together, let us explore the meaning of Peter's designated

name, "Cephas." Referring only to John's Gospel, we know that Peter's birth name was "Simon." With one exception, Luke wrote that his name was "Simeon." During the time of Jesus, many Jewish parents named their sons Simon; it was a common name. However, as it pertains to Jona's son, we turn to Elder Talmage and read these explanatory words: "The significance of names when given of God finds illustration in many scriptural instances." Providing several illustrations, he points out that "'Simon,' meaning a *hearer*, the name of the man who became the chief apostle of Jesus Christ, was changed by the Lord to 'Cephas' (Aramaic) or 'Peter' (Greek) meaning a *rock*"[50] (italics in quotation).

Describing what the Savior said to Peter, Elder Talmage has further written: "Thou art Simon the son of Jona; thou shalt be called 'Cephas.' The new name thus bestowed is the Aramaic or Syro-Chaldaic equivalent of the Greek 'Petros,' and of the present English 'Peter,' meaning 'a stone.'"[51]

With a different point of view, Alfred Edersheim also quotes what the Savior said when he saw Peter: "Thou art Simon, the son of John [*sic*]—thou shalt be called Cephas, which is interpreted (Grecian-ised) [*sic*] Peter." Regarding the name of Peter's father, he wrote, "So according to the best text, [John] and not Jona." Regarding Peter's name, he explains, "So in the Greek, of which the English interpretation is 'a *stone*'— *Keyph*, or *Keypha*, 'a rock'"[52] (italics in quotation).

With yet another understanding, Farrar also quotes what the Savior said to Peter: "Thou art Simon, the son of Jona; thou shalt be called Kephas;' that is, 'Thou art Simon, the son of the *dove*; hereafter thou shalt be as the rock in which the dove hides'"[53] (italics included in quotation).

"A SEER, OR A STONE"
(JST John 1: 42)

From the Joseph Smith Translation of John, the following information is revealed: "And he [Andrew] brought him [Peter] to Jesus. And when Jesus beheld him, he said, Thou art Simon, the son of Jona, thou shalt be called Cephas, which is, by interpretation, a seer, or a stone . . . ."

Based upon this scripture, Elder McConkie has penned these declarative words: "And so Andrew brought Simon—Simon Peter!—unto Jesus. Jesus said: 'Thou art Simon, the son of Jona, thou shalt be called Cephas.' This new name—'which is, by interpretation, a seer, or a stone'—forecast what was to be in the life of Andrew's brother, who was destined to be, under the Lord, the chief officer of the perfected church and kingdom, the foundations of which were then being laid. Peter, the Rock and the Seer, who would yet hold the keys of the kingdom of heaven . . . ."[54]

Though there are differing opinions among our recognized scholars, the general consensus seems to indicate that *Cephas* means *Peter*, which is, by interpretation, a *rock*. Most importantly, from the Prophet Joseph Smith, we know that it means a "seer, or a stone." Therefore, Simon's new name was designated *Peter*.

"SIMON CALLED PETER"
(Matt. 4: 18; 10: 2; Mark 1: 16, 29; Luke 6: 14; John 1: 40; 6: 8; 1 Peter 1:1; 2 Peter 1: 1)

Though the Savior designated Simon's name to be Peter, the Gospel writers continued to periodically refer to him by his birth name. From Matthew we read, "Simon called Peter."

36

Mark wrote that Jesus "saw Simon and Andrew his brother." Luke also has written, "Simon (whom he also named Peter) and Andrew his brother." From John, we read these words, "Andrew, Simon Peter's brother." With interest, we read that Simon, himself, in his First Epistle, wrote these introductory words: "Peter, an apostle of Jesus Christ." Then, in his Second Epistle, he says, "Simon Peter, a servant and an apostle of Jesus Christ."

After meeting the Savior and hearing those memorable words, "Thou art Simon, the son of Jona, thou shalt be called Cephas," Peter now believed, as did his brother, Andrew, that Jesus truly was the Son of God. There was no need for a long conversion process; no need to ponder and pray for an answer; immediately, with the aid of the Spirit, Peter received the sure witness that Jesus was the Messiah.

THE BROTHERS FOLLOWED JESUS
(JST 1: 42)

Peter and Andrew, and James and John, had met the Savior. Each brother was taught the gospel of Jesus Christ. By the Spirit, individually and collectively, these new disciples knew whom they would follow. The completeness and surety of their conversion is attested to in the words found in the Joseph Smith Translation of John: "And they were fishermen. And they straightway left all, and followed Jesus."

Elder McConkie has well explained: "Such is the mark of valiant souls who know whereof they speak. These disciples had testimonies of the truth and divinity of the work from the very day they met and were taught by the Lord Jesus. Thereafter they would be fed spiritually by his teachings and his deeds, but from the beginning they were forsaking all to follow him. Even their daily bread and that of their families must somehow be supplied by other means; they are laying down their nets to commence a work that will make them fishers of men."[55]

WERE THE DISCIPLES MARRIED?
(Matt. 8:5, 14; Mark 1:21; Luke 4:31,38)

From what Elder McConkie has written, "Even their daily bread and that of their families must somehow be supplied by other means," it is proper to wonder about the marital status of these new disciples. As with numerous personal matters, the Gospel writers have not revealed whether or not the new disciples were married, excepting that of Peter.

DUTY REQUIREMENTS OF JEWISH MALES

From Farrar, we discover that there were certain duty requirements of male members of the Jewish race: "According to Juda Ben Tema, at *five* he was to study the Scriptures (Mikra), at ten the Mishna, at thirteen the Talmud; *at eighteen he was to marry*, at twenty to acquire riches, at thirty strength, at forty prudence, and so on to the end"[56] (italics in quotation).

In almost the same order, Edersheim has penned similar expressions. Pertaining to the marital age of a Jewish man, our Jewish scholar has written:

". . . at eighteen years, marriage . . . ."[57]

Therefore, from these noted scholars, of over a hundred years past, it appears that the standard age of a Jewish man to marry was at or around eighteen. We now turn our attention to the marital ages of Jewish women.

MARITAL AGES OF JEWISH WOMEN

With another understanding, Elder McConkie has written:

"Men married at sixteen or seventeen years of age, almost never later than twenty; and women at a somewhat younger age, often when not older than fourteen. These ages applied to all . . . ."[58]

Based upon what has been written by our recognized scholars, we are safe to believe that in addition to Peter, Andrew, James and John were also married and that each brother had children. In support of this belief, we use the words of Elder McConkie: "These brethren were not novices; the gospel message was not new to them . . . . But with it all, they still needed bread to fill their own bellies, fish to fill the mouths of their wives and children, money to support their families."[59]

THE FAMILIES OF THE DISCIPLES
(Eph. 3: 15; JST 1: 42; Matt. 4: 18-21; Mark 1: 16-20; Luke 5: 1-10)

As it is in heaven so it is upon this earth: the family is the basic unit of the Church. The family is so important that The First Presidency and Council of the Twelve Apostles of The Church of Jesus Christ of Latter-day Saints issued a marvelous document, *A Proclamation To The World.* In it, we read important doctrines about God's law, especially about marriage, chastity, and taking care of children. It emphasizes strongly the family unit is approved by God, and that marriage is a necessary part of Heavenly Father's plan (delivered September 23, 1995, by President Gordon B. Hinckley).[60]

With this statement, we know that our Lord did not call his disciples to follow him and forsake their families. We wonder what the new converts said to their individual families concerning leaving the fishing business and following the Messiah. Although not written by the gospel writers, would it

39

be unreasonable to believe that the Savior met with the families of the disciples and explained why he called them? Just like the disciples, we can safely believe that their wives and children also had "believing blood" flowing in their veins. Neither husbands nor wives can serve effectively in the Church without the support of their spouses and children. Whatever transpired, we read from the Joseph Smith Translation of John: "And they—Peter, Andrew, James, and John—straightway left all, and followed Jesus."

The Lord has revealed the following doctrine regarding the financial support of families: "Women have claim on their husbands for their maintenance, until their husbands are taken .... All children have claim upon their parents for their maintenance until they are of age. And after that, they have claim upon the church, or in other words upon the Lord's storehouse, if their parents have not wherewith to give them inheritances . . ." (See D&C 83: 2-5).

We know that Peter, Andrew, James, and John had the financial means to provide "maintenance" for their individual families. Accordingly, we repeat the words written by Elder McConkie, "Even their daily bread and that of their families must somehow be supplied by other means." By reason that these disciples were wealthy fishing partners, we may properly suppose that Zebedee, who was the father of James and John, continued their commercial fishing business. Therefore, he was the individual who, in their absence, "supplied" the "means" for the families of the disciples of Jesus.

PETER, THE SEER

As Elder McConkie has previously written, Simon will be known as "Peter, the Rock and the Seer." Peter's testimony is now as firm as a "rock." Then, while serving in the First Presidency, he would be the prophet, "seer," and revelator for the whole Church.

Chapter Ten

APOSTLES, PROPHETS, SEERS, AND REVELATORS

From ancient times until the present, the members of the First Presidency and the Quorum of the Twelve are sustained as prophet, seers, and revelators. Such was the case with Peter, Andrew, James, and John.

OFFICERS IN THE CHURCH
(Eph. 4: 11-13)

In his Epistle to the Ephesians, Paul wrote this information about the officers in Christ's true Church: "And he gave some, apostles; and some, prophets; and some, evangelists; and some, pastors and teachers; For the perfecting of the saints, for the work of the ministry, for the edifying of the body of Christ: Till we all come in the unity of the faith, and of the knowledge of the Son of God, unto a perfect man, unto the measure of the stature of the fulness of Christ."

APOSTLES
(Heb. 3: 1; D&C 107: 23, 33)

Because twelve men—who were Peter, Andrew, James, and John, plus eight other men—were ordained apostles by our Lord, let us find out the meaning of the word *apostle*. Elder Talmage says, "The word 'apostle' is an Anglicized form derived from the Greek *apostolos*, meaning literally 'one who is sent,' and connoting an envoy or official messenger, who speaks and acts by the authority of one superior to himself. In this sense Paul afterward applied the title to Christ as one specially sent and commissioned of the Father"[61] (italics included in quotation).

Then, from Elder McConkie, we learn the significance of this holy calling: "This is the supreme office in the church in all dispensations because those so ordained hold both the fulness of the priesthood and all of the keys of the kingdom of God on earth. The President of the Church serves in that high and exalted position because he is the senior apostle of God on earth and thus can direct the manner in which all other apostles and priesthood holders use their priesthood."[62]

Though Peter was designated by our Lord to be a seer, he was not yet called to the apostleship. In a future day, Peter would serve as the "President of the Church" and preside as "the senior apostle of God on earth."

Regarding those individuals who are called to be apostles, we rely again upon Elder McConkie for information: "An apostle is an ordained office in the Melchizedek Priesthood, and those so ordained . . . are set apart as members of the Quorum of the Twelve and are given the keys and power to preside over the church and kingdom and regulate all of the affairs of God on earth."[63]

In harmony with what Elder Talmage wrote—that an apostle is "one who is sent," Elder McConkie explains, quoting: "Apostles are 'special witnesses of the name of Christ in all the world.' They are also 'a Traveling Presiding High Council, to officiate in the name of the Lord, under the direction of the Presidency of the Church, agreeable to the institution of heaven; to build up the church, and regulate all the affairs of the same in all nations, first unto the Gentiles and secondly unto the Jews.'"[64]

Therefore, Peter—just like those who are called to be an apostle in our dispensation—was to be a "special witness of the name of Christ" and was to "build up the church, and regulate all the affairs of the same in all nations." We now turn our attention to "prophets."

PROPHETS
(Numbers 11: 29; Rev. 19: 10)

Considering prophets, we rely again upon Elder McConkie for information: "Next to apostles come prophets. They are persons who have 'the testimony of Jesus,' which 'is the spirit of prophecy' . . . . The prophetic position is not an ordained office in the priesthood, although every person who holds the priesthood is or should be a prophet . . . . The First Presidency and the Twelve are sustained as prophets, seers, and revelators to the church. The President is the presiding prophet on earth and as such is the one through whom revelation is sent forth to the world and for the guidance of the whole body of believing saints."[65]

Later, Peter would serve in the First Presidency with the brothers James and John. Simon Peter would be the "presiding prophet on earth and as such [would be] the one through whom revelation [would be] sent forth to the world." Next, let us learn why Peter was called by our Lord to be a "seer."

SEERS
(Mosiah 8: 13-18; Matt. 16: 18)

"Seers," explains Elder McConkie, "are specially selected prophets who are authorized to use the Urim and Thummim and who are empowered to know past, present, and future things. 'A gift which is greater can no man have.'"[66]

As it pertains to Peter, Elder McConkie says, "Added significance will soon be given this designation when, in promising him the keys of the kingdom, our Lord will tell Peter that the gates of hell shall never prevail against the rock of revelation, or in other words against seership."[67]

REVELATORS
(D&C 77:2; 100: 11; 128: 6; D&C 107: 92; 124: 94, 125)

Regarding a revelator, Elder McConkie provides this information: "Anyone who receives revelation from the Lord and conveys the revealed truth to another is a *revelator*. Joseph Smith was a revelator to Sidney Rigdon; the beloved disciple, because of the great revelations he left for the world, is known as John the Revelator. The President of the Church is a revelator for the Church, as also are the members of the First Presidency, [and] the Council of the Twelve . . ."[68] (italics in quotation).

PETER TO BE THE PRESIDENT OF THE CHURCH

To repeat, when Simon Peter was called by the Lord to be a seer, he was not yet called to the apostleship. When he was officially called to serve in the Twelve, he was the senior member. By virtue that he was the senior apostle, Peter became the President of the Church, following the death of Jesus; therefore, he became the prophet, seer, and revelator for the whole Church.

Chapter Eleven

JESUS CALLED OTHER DISCIPLES

PETER AND HIS FELLOW DISCIPLES
(John 1: 37-42)

After Peter and Andrew, and James and John, were called by our Lord to be disciples, they met and traveled with other disciples who were also called by Jesus. Because these new disciples closely associated with Simon Peter, this chapter will briefly present information regarding their individual calls.

As has been written earlier in this work, Andrew and his fishing partner, John, became disciples of our Lord. Then, Andrew found his brother, Simon, and brought him to meet the Messiah. Therefore, *Simon called Peter* also became a disciple of our Lord. Accordingly, these three individuals are credited as being the first disciples of Jesus.

Let us consider another point of view. After our Lord designated Simon's name to be Peter, Edersheim has written these believable words: "It must not, of course, be supposed that this represents all that had passed between Jesus and Peter, any more than that the recorded expression was all that Andrew and John had said of Jesus to their brothers. Of the interview between John and James his brother, the writer, with his usual self-reticence [inclined to be silent], forbears to speak. But we know its result; and, knowing it, can form some conception of what passed on that holy evening between the new-found Messiah and His *first four disciples* . . ."[69] (italics added).

47

In agreement with there being "four disciples," Farrar states that when Philip was called by our Lord to be a disciple that "a fifth neophyte [a new convert] was added to that sacred and happy band."[70]

Relying again upon Edersheim, we read these truth-filled words: "As yet they were only followers, learners, not yet called to be Apostles."[71]

JESUS WENT TO GALILEE
(John 1: 28, 43)

Following his stay in Bethabara, we learn that Jesus was desirous to return to Galilee. To understand why he traveled toward this area along with his new converts, we use the paraphrased words of Edersheim: For his sake and those of his new disciples, Jesus traveled to Jerusalem for his first visit, as the Messiah, to attend the Paschal Feast.[72] (Regarding this feast, See Notes 1 and 2, end of chapter.)

It is important to know that Jesus did not travel with his new disciples solely to attend the "Paschal Feast;" his main purpose for going was to call two more followers. From John's Gospel, we discover that Philip was the next disciple.

PHILIP
(John 1: 43)

John says, "The day following Jesus would go forth into Galilee, and findeth Philip, and saith unto him, Follow me."

Regarding Philip, Farrar states: "On the fourth day He [Jesus] wished to start for His return to Galilee, and on the journey fell in with another young fisherman, Philip of Bethsaida."[73]

From Elder Talmage, we gather this information: "*Philip*

may have been the first to receive the authoritative call 'Follow me' from the lips of Jesus, and we find him immediately testifying that Jesus was the long expected Messiah . . . . It is said that Jesus found him, whereas the others concerned in that early affiliation seem to have come of themselves severally to Christ"[74] (italics in quotation).

While traveling from Bethabara to Bethsaida, we wonder where Jesus and his new disciples found lodging for the evening. Further, whether they brought their own food or obtained it by purchase. Whatever transpired during this journey, we can be assured that the physical and spiritual needs of Peter and his colleagues were sufficiently met.

PHILIP'S CONVERSION
(John 1: 43)

As with all new converts, what causes an individual to believe the doctrines of a particular church? Though each conversion story is unique, generally speaking, an individual has to be taught the gospel. Whether those doctrines are written or verbally spoken, a person gains a testimony of the truthfulness of the message.

The following day, Jesus and his disciples traveled to a city in Galilee, called Bethsaida. While there, Jesus found Philip and said unto him, "Follow me." We may properly believe that our Lord, along with Peter—the newly designated seer—and his fellow disciples, told Philip all that had transpired in recent days. Further, they taught him the gospel and, each in turn, bore personal testimony of Jesus' divinity.

Those individuals who have gained a testimony of the truthfulness of the gospel from listening to the testimony of others can, in some degree, appreciate how Philip gained his testimony. It is important to point out that he was not in atten-

49

dance at an ordinary testimony meeting. Jesus, himself, and four of the greatest of all men, were bearing testimony to him.

NATHANAEL
(Matt. 10: 3; John 1: 45-46)

Now that Philip had come into the fold, what did he do next? As should be the case with all new converts, he desired to share his testimony. Philip shared his testimony with a friend, Nathanael, who is believed to be Bartholomew, the apostle. With a burning testimony, and with conviction, Philip said, "We have found him, of whom Moses in the law, and the prophets, did write, Jesus of Nazareth, the son of Joseph."

Not in the spirit of doubt or skepticism, but using a derogatory proverb of the day, Nathanael replied, "Can there any good thing come out of Nazareth?" With a persuasive invitation, Philip answered, "Come and see."

NATHANAEL'S CONVERSION
(John 1: 47-51; Deut. 32: 4; D&C 84: 102; 109: 77; Alma 5: 48; 9: 26; 13: 9)

The conversion process was taking place in Nathanael's life and he accepted the invitation of Philip to meet "Jesus of Nazareth." Picture these two friends walking toward the band of believers, and upon seeing Nathanael, Jesus spoke these startling words, "Behold an Israelite indeed, in whom is no guile!"

Whether out of curiosity, or reacting naturally, Nathanael asked, "Whence knowest thou me?" Exhibiting the gift of seership—a gift that allows an individual to know past, present, or future events—our Lord explained, "Before that Philip called thee, when thou was under the fig tree, I saw thee." Evidently, he had undergone some spiritual experience while praying, or meditating, under a fig tree. Probably, our Lord revealed to his future apostle what had actually taken place under the tree. The disciples—who were Peter, Andrew, John, James, and Philip—individually bore their testimonies to this man, in order that he might understand gospel truths. All this, along with Jesus' seeric declaration, caused the guileless Nathanael to exclaim: "Rabbi, thou art the Son of God; thou art the King of Israel."

Fortunately for us, this was not the end of the conversation between Nathanael and Jesus. Our Lord then asked this thought-provoking question, "Because I said unto thee, I saw thee under the fig tree, believest thou?" Without waiting for a response, our Lord gave him this marvelous promise: "Thou shalt see greater things than these." Jesus then foretold what would happen in a future day. "Verily, verily, I say unto you, Hereafter ye shall see heaven open, and the angels of God ascending and descending upon the Son of Man."

As to when this marvelous manifestation transpired, the gospel writers do not inform us. We can be assured that it did transpire, for all of the words promised by our Lord are fulfilled, for Jesus is a God of truth.

Imagine the thoughts that must have passed through Peter's mind, and those of his fellow disciples, when our Lord revealed to Nathanael about his experience under a fig tree. Further, how each must have felt spiritually when Jesus promised this new disciple a future angelic manifestation. In conclusion, as it pertains to the early ministry of Jesus, he was teaching the gospel, calling disciples to forsake their vocations, and asking them to follow him. Because they had strong testimonies that Jesus was the Christ, Peter, Andrew, James, John, Philip, and Nathanael became faithful followers of our Lord.

NOTES
(Deut. 16: 1-6; Exo. 12: 2; Josephus; *Wars of the Jews*, ii, 1: 3;
Jesus the Christ, pp. 112-113)

1. It is noted that the Paschal Feast and the Passover feast are one in the same. Regarding this feast, we begin by using the words of Elder Talmage:

"This religious festival, it should be remembered, was one of the most solemn and sacred among the many ceremonial commemorations of the Jews; it had been established at the time of the peoples' exodus from Egypt, in remembrance of the outstretched arm of power by which God had delivered Israel after the angel of destruction had slain the firstborn in every Egyptian home and had mercifully passed over the houses of the children of Jacob. It was of such importance that its annual recurrence was made the beginning of the new year. The Law required all males to present themselves before the Lord at the feast. The rule was that women should likewise attend if not lawfully detained . . . .

"The feast proper lasted seven days, and in the time of Christ was annually attended by great concourses of Jews; Josephus speaks of such a Passover gathering as 'an innumerable multitude.' The people came from distant provinces in large companies and caravans, as a matter of convenience and as a means of common protection against the marauding bands which are known to have infested the country."

2. From Frederic W. Farrar, pages 423, 511-512, we gather this information about the last Passover of Jesus, and the symbolism between our Lord and the Paschal lamb that was eaten at this feast:

"If the customs enjoined by the Law had been capable of rigid and exact fulfillment, the Paschal lamb for the use of Himself and His disciples would have been set apart on the previous Sunday evening; but although, since the days of the exile the Passover had been observed, it is probable that the changed circumstances of the nation had introduced many natural and perfectly justifiable changes in the old regulations. It would have been a simple impossibility for the myriads of pilgrims to provide themselves beforehand with a Paschal Lamb.

". . . He, the true Paschal Lamb, was to be sacrificed once and forever in the Holy City [Jerusalem], where it is probable that in that very Passover, and on the very same day, some 260,000 of those lambs of which He was the antitype were destined to be slain."

Chapter Twelve

THE MARRIAGE IN CANA

PETER AND HIS FELLOW DISCIPLES
ATTENDED THE MARRIAGE
(John 2: 1-12; Heb. 13: 4; Matt. 19: 4-9)

Turning our attention to a happening in a place called Cana, we are informed by John that on the third day of the week, "there was a marriage in Cana of Galilee; and the mother of Jesus was there." Further, that "Jesus was called, and his disciples, to the marriage." John does not inform us by whom or when Jesus and Peter and his fellow disciples were "called" and expected to be in attendance at the wedding. We only know that they were at the wedding. It is noteworthy that our Savior's presence at this particular festivity is evidence of the divine approval of marriages and their related activities.

Regarding this wedding, the consensus of our recognized scholars is that Mary's active part in providing for the needs of the wedding guests indicates that one of her children was being married.[75]

MARY'S REQUEST
(John 2: 3)

Frederic W. Farrar informs us that marriage festivities of the time could last up to a week.[76] According to John's record, sometime during the end of the celebration, "the mother of

55

Jesus saith unto him, They have no wine." From Mary's words, we can surmise what she expected her distinguished son to do: To provide the needed wine for the wedding guests; not by purchase, but by the use of his divine power.

RESPONSE OF JESUS
(John 2: 4-5)

Our attention is now turned to the Messiah and his response. In unmistakable tones of authority, yet with respect, our Lord spoke these words of mild reproof: "Woman, what have I to do with thee? mine hour is not yet come." From these words, we can surmise what Jesus was saying: "Mother, no longer am I under your parental care or authority. I am on my Father's business, and I will determine the time and the place for performing miracles."

After receiving his reproof, Mary, because of her faith in her divine Son, knew that her request would be granted. Accordingly, she said to the servants, "Whatsoever he saith unto you, do it."

"WOMAN"

Regarding Jesus calling his mother, "Woman," Elder Talmage explains: "The noun of address, 'Woman,' as applied by a son to his mother may sound to our ears somewhat harsh, if not disrespectful; but its use was really an expression of opposite import." In a footnote, Elder Talmage quotes the expression of Farrar: "The address 'Woman' was so respectful that it might be, and was, addressed to the queenliest."[77]

WATER TURNED INTO WINE
(John 2: 6-11)

Jesus had the servants fill six empty waterpots full with water. Each pot held from "two or three firkins apiece" of water. A firkin is equivalent to nine gallons. As soon as the containers were filled to the brim, our Lord asked those same servants to draw from a vessel and give a taste of the contents to the governor of the feast. Upon tasting the wine, this honored guest responded: "Every man at the beginning doth set forth good wine; and when men have well drunk, then that which is worse: but thou hast kept the good wine until now." From the short time that the waterpots were filled with water until the servants drew it out, approximately 150 gallons of "good wine" had been produced. Whether Jesus spoke any words or simply willed it to be done, we are not informed. Whatever transpired at this event, the miracle occurred.

We can well imagine what the wedding guests said to one another upon learning from the servants how the wine was furnished. From this same record, we discover that this was the beginning of Jesus' miracles. Further, that this act "manifested forth his glory; and his disciples believed on him."

"HIS DISCIPLES BELIEVED ON HIM"
(John 2: 11)

Though John wrote "his disciples believed on him," it is important to point out that prior to this miracle being performed, Peter and his fellow disciples believed that Jesus was the Messiah. Previously, we learned how they gained their testimonies. This miracle only verified and increased their belief that Jesus truly was the Christ.

PETER MET JESUS' FAMILY
(Matt. 13: 54-56)

Because Peter and his fellow disciples were at the marriage of one of Mary's children, they became acquainted with Jesus' immediate family. Since Joseph is not mentioned at the marriage in Cana or throughout the rest of the New Testament it is assumed that he is dead.[78] Therefore, Peter and his colleagues never met Mary's husband. However, they met our Lord's half-brothers, and more than likely his half-sisters. From Matthew's Gospel, we know that Joseph and Mary had at least four sons and more than one daughter. We read that when our Savior's formal ministry began, the people in Nazareth "were astonished, and said, Whence hath this man this wisdom, and these mighty works? Is not this the carpenter's son? is not his mother called Mary? and his brethren, James, and Joses, and Simon, and Judas? And his sisters, are they not all with us? Whence then hath this man all these things?"

THE "BRETHREN" OF JESUS
(Mark 6: 3; Jude 1: 1; John 2: 12; 7: 5; Luke 2: 34-35; Matt 12: 46; 13:55; 1 Cor. 9: 5; Acts 1:14; Gal. 1: 19)

Mark's Gospel also names the Lord's half-brothers, with one exception: He writes the name of Juda instead of Judas. In the epistle of Jude, this half-brother of Jesus refers to himself as "Jude, the servant of Jesus Christ, and brother of James . . ." Though there appears to be three separate names—Judas, Juda, Jude—the general view is that they are one in the same person. In addition, we are not informed from the scriptures the names of Jesus' sisters or the exact number. However, we know that he had at least two half-sisters, perhaps more.

Although children may be raised under one roof by the

same parents, each child reacts to their parents' teaching and influence unlike that of his fellow siblings. Such seems to be the case with Jesus and his half-brothers. We learn from the apostle John that during most of our Lord's ministry, his sibling brothers did not have a testimony that he was the Savior and Redeemer of the world. The record states, "For neither did his brethren believe in him."

Regarding this scripture, we use the thoughts and words of Elder McConkie: "Frequent special reference is made to the sons of Joseph and Mary as the 'brethren' of Jesus, though in fact they were his half-brothers. Though they were reared in the same household and came under the benign influence of Joseph and Mary, though they were aware of the teachings, ministry, and miracles of Jesus himself, yet these his close relatives had not so far accepted him as the Messiah. However, all of them, apparently, were converted later; one of them, identified by Paul as 'James the Lord's brother' was to minister in the holy apostleship; and yet another, Judas, who calls himself, 'Jude the . . . brother of James,' wrote the epistle of Jude."[79]

As it pertains to Jesus' half-sisters, we are not informed how they believed or if they were like unto their brothers. We can only trust that if they did not at first believe that their older brother was the Christ, they also "were converted later."

This truly must have been a challenging and troubling situation for Mary and Joseph to have all of Jesus' half-brothers not believe their words regarding the divinity of Jesus. As Simeon explained to her in the temple, Mary was experiencing the "sword" of grief and sorrow because of her own unconverted sons. This situation continued for nearly thirty-three years. As is the case with many good and faithful parents of disbelieving or wayward children, all that a mother or father can do is love them and sincerely pray that one day those sons or daughters will see the light and change their thinking and actions. Finally, after years of instruction, long-suffering, patience, tears, and prayer, Mary's doubting sons were converted. We do not know what caused their conversion; only that they finally became faithful and believing members. Finally, because of the conversion of her former disbelieving sons, this devoted mother experienced joy and peace of mind.

Following the wedding, Peter and his fellow disciples traveled with Jesus to Capernaum. Together, let us learn what happened in this place.

Chapter Thirteen

PETER AND HIS FELLOW DISCIPLES
WENT TO CAPERNAUM
(John 2: 12; Matt. 9: 1)

Following the miracle at Cana, a day or two later, Peter and his fellow disciples went with Jesus and his half-brothers and their mother, Mary, to the city of Capernaum. Regarding this city, Elder Talmage has written: ". . . a town pleasantly situated near the northernly end of the Sea of Galilee or Lake of Gennesaret and the scene of many of our Lord's miraculous works; indeed it came to be known as His own city. Because of the unbelief of its people it became a subject of lamentation to Jesus when in sorrow He prefigured the judgment that would befall the place."[80]

From Farrar, we gather the following information about this place: "That little city was Capernaum. It rose under the gentle declivities (sloping down) of hills that encircled an earthly Paradise. There were no such trees, and no such gardens, anywhere in Palestine as in the land of Gennesareth. The very name means 'garden of abundance,' and the numberless flowers blossom over a little plain which is in 'sight like unto an emerald.' It was doubtless a part of Christ's divine plan that His ministry should begin amid scenes so beautiful, and that the good tidings, which revealed to mankind their loftiest hopes and purest pleasures, should be first proclaimed in a region of unusual loveliness."[81]

MARY LIVED IN CAPERNAUM

Turning our attention to the mother of our Lord, we may believe that in addition to Mary's loyalty in following Jesus to Capernaum, Elder McConkie has written that we may "suppose" that she and her sons from Joseph also resided in this town.[82] Elder McConkie's supposition seems logical since Joseph was no longer alive. It is reasonable to believe that sometime after Joseph's death, Mary disposed of the home in Nazareth and moved her family to be closer to her eldest son.

PETER LIVED IN CAPERNAUM
(Matt. 8: 5, 14; Mark 1: 21, 29; Luke 4: 31, 38)

In addition to Mary and her sons living in Capernaum, we understand that Peter was also living in Capernaum with his wife and his wife's mother. Together, let us discover if other disciples lived in Capernaum.

OTHER DISCIPLES LIVED IN CAPERNAUM
(Matt. 8: 14; Luke 4: 38; Mark 1: 29; Matt. 9: 1, 9; Mark 2: 1, 14; Luke 5: 27)

When Peter's mother-in-law was ill with a "great fever," both Matthew and Luke have written that Jesus entered into "Peter's house." However, Mark says, "they [Jesus and his disciples] entered into the house of Simon and Andrew, with James and John." Whether or not Andrew lived in Peter's home, or was a co-owner, we are left to wonder. From what Matthew and Luke have written, it seems reasonable to believe that Peter had a home separate from Andrew's, in the same city of Capernaum.

Without providing the references, Elder McConkie has

written that Capernaum "was the home of Peter and Andrew, and of James and John, and that it was the place where Matthew sat as a collector of customs."[83]

PETER WENT TO THE PASSOVER IN JERUSALEM
(John 2: 12-17)

As the Passover was about to begin, we read that this small group of people "continued there not many days" in Capernaum. Although the next verse states "Jesus went up to Jerusalem," it appears consistent with custom, and the preceding scripture, that all of the individuals in this group went with our Lord to observe the Paschal festival together. It was at this yearly observance that our Lord, by physical force and righteous indignation, cleared the temple for the first time. We may well believe that Peter and his fellow disciples were able to see for the first time the righteous anger of Jesus, and the use of his physical strength to teach all that this was his "Father's house" and that he was his Father's Son!

PETER WAS PRESENT WHEN
JESUS TAUGHT HIS OWN RESURRECTION
(John 2: 18-22)

While at the temple, the Jews approached our Lord and asked, "What sign shewest thou unto us, seeing that thou doest these things?" Answering, he said, "Destroy this temple, and in three days I will raise it up." Not understanding, some of the individuals replied that it took forty-six years to build that house. As John explains, "But he spake of the temple of his body." Then, after Jesus was resurrected, John writes "his disciples—who were Peter, Andrew, James, John, Philip, and

Nathanael—remembered that he had said this unto them; and they believed the scripture, and the word which Jesus had said."

JESUS AND NICODEMUS
(John 3: 1-7)

After our Lord cleared the temple, we find out that a member of the "Pharisees, named Nicodemus, a ruler of the Jews" visited "Jesus by night, and said unto him, Rabbi, we know that thou art a teacher come from God: for no man can do these miracles that thou doest, except God be with him."

From Elder Talmage, we learn what was discussed during this visit: "Without waiting for specific questions, 'Jesus answered and said unto him, Verily, verily, I say unto thee, Except a man be born again, he cannot see the kingdom of God.' Nicodemus appears to have been puzzled; he asked how such a rejuvenation was possible. 'How can a man be born when he is old? can he enter the second time into his mother's womb, and be born?' . . .

"Jesus repeated the declaration, and with precision, emphasizing by the impressive 'Verily, verily,' the greatest lesson that had ever saluted the ears of this ruler in Israel: 'Verily, verily, I say unto thee, Except a man be born of water and of the Spirit, he cannot enter into the kingdom of God.' That the new birth thus declared to be absolutely essential as a condition of entrance into the kingdom of God, applicable to every man, without limitation or qualification, was a spiritual regeneration, was next explained to the wondering Rabbi: 'That which is born of the flesh is flesh; and that which is born of the Spirit is spirit. Marvel not that I said unto thee, Ye must be born again.'"[84]

THE IMPORTANCE OF GOSPEL ORDINANCES

To emphasize the importance of this conversation between our Lord and the Pharisee ruler, we again use the words of Elder Talmage: "The narrative of this interview between Nicodemus and the Christ constitutes one of our most instructive and precious scriptures relating to the absolute necessity of unreserved compliance with the laws and ordinances of the gospel, as the means indispensable to salvation. Faith in Jesus Christ as the Son of God, through whom alone men may gain eternal life; the forsaking of sin by resolute turning away from the gross darkness of evil to the saving light of righteousness; the unqualified requirement of a new birth through baptism in water, and this of necessity by the mode of immersion, since otherwise the figure of a birth would be meaningless; and the completion of the new birth through baptism by the Spirit—all these principles are taught herein in such simplicity and plainness as to make plausible no man's excuse for ignorance."[85]

JOHN, THE DISCIPLE

Regarding the conversation between Jesus and Nicodemus, Elder Talmage provides this information about John, the disciple: "If Jesus and Nicodemus were the only persons present at the interview, John, the writer, must have been informed thereof by one of the two. As John was one of the early disciples, afterwards one of the apostles, and as he was distinguished in the apostolic company by his close personal companionship with the Lord, it is highly probable that he heard the account from the lips of Jesus. It was evidently John's purpose to record the great lesson of the occasion rather than to tell the circumstantial story. The record begins and ends with equal abruptness; unimportant incidents are omitted; every line is of significance; the writer fully realized the deep import of his subject and treated it accordingly."[86]

DID JOHN INFORM PETER?

Because "this interview between Nicodemus and the Christ constitutes one of our most instructive and precious scriptures relating to the absolute necessity of unreserved compliance with the laws and ordinances of the gospel," we may properly suppose that John informed Peter, and his fellow disciples, of this glorious conversation. We may further suppose, shortly thereafter, that Jesus also taught his newly-called disciples the same doctrines that were plainly explained to Nicodemus.

THE LORD'S HALF-BROTHERS
(Acts 1: 14; Gal. 1: 19; Jude 1)

We now turn our attention to the Lord's half-brothers. It is noted that while at the marriage in Cana and at the Passover, these close relatives of our Lord did not believe that Jesus was the Messiah. However, though they were at that time unbelievers, it is important to be aware that they were good and honorable men. In support of this statement, we use the quoted words of Elder McConkie: "However, all of them, apparently, were converted later; one of them, identified by Paul as 'James the Lord's brother,' was to minister in the holy apostleship; and yet another, Judas, who calls himself, 'Jude the . . . brother of James,' wrote the epistle of Jude."

APOSTLES ARE CALLED BY INSPIRATION

Concerning James, our Lord's half-brother, we know that from the days of Adam to our present time, every man who has been ordained an apostle was called by inspiration. To support

66

this declaration, we turn our attention to our modern time when President Heber J. Grant called a comparative stranger to be an apostle.

"A COMPARATIVE STRANGER"

From Elder Spencer W. Kimball, we gather the following information: "During the years he was a member of the Council of the Twelve, President Heber J. Grant often recommended names of brethren to the First Presidency for consideration as apostles. Frequently he thought that if he ever were President of the Church he would appoint his life-long friend, General Richard W. Young, a grandson of President Brigham Young, to the apostleship. However, when he did become President he chose instead, under the inspiration of the Lord, a relative stranger to him, Elder Melvin J. Ballard."[87]

Without mentioning his name, President Grant, in a General Conference, revealed the following information about Elder Ballard: "I have been happy during the twenty-two years that it has fallen my lot to stand at the head of this Church. I have felt the inspiration of the Living God directing me in my labors. From the day that I chose a comparative stranger to be one of the Apostles, instead of my lifelong and dearest living friend, I have known as I know that I live, that I am entitled to the light and the inspiration and the guidance of God in directing His work here upon this earth . . . ."[88]

With this statement, we again return to the half-brother of Jesus. It was not by coincidence that Peter and his fellow disciples became acquainted with these close relatives of our Lord at the marriage in Cana, and at the Passover. Concerning James being called to the apostleship, we wonder about his association with Peter.

PETER AND JAMES
(Acts 12: 1-17; 15: 6-21)

Comparing what President Grant said about Elder Ballard, we do not know whether James became Peter's "dearest living friend," or was to him "a comparative stranger." The only information we have is that Peter, as the President of the Church, called James, by inspiration, to be an apostle.

The following event transpired approximately eleven years after Jesus was crucified: "Now about that time that Herod the king stretched forth his hands to vex certain [leaders] of the church. And he killed James the brother of John with the sword."

Tragically, one of Peter's counselors in the First Presidency had been slain. By reason that a vacancy occurred in the First Presidency, Peter, by inspiration, called James, the Lord's brother, to be his new counselor. Shortly after "James the brother of John" had been slain, Peter, himself, was put in "prison." By divine intervention, an angel of the Lord freed Peter from his captors.

At the "house of Mary the mother of John, whose surname was Mark; where many were gathered together praying," Peter said to the people, "Go shew these things [explain what had just transpired] unto James, and to the brethren [who were the apostles]. And he departed, and went into another place."

After Paul was made an apostle, he explains: "Neither went I up to Jerusalem to them which were apostles before me; but I went into Arabia, and returned again unto Damascus. Then after three years I went up to Jerusalem to see Peter, and abode with him fifteen days. But other of the apostles saw I none, save James the Lord's brother" (See Gal. 1: 17-19).

In the first half of Acts, John, the other counselor in the First Presidency, appears prominently with Peter. In the

68

second half of Acts, James, the Lord's brother, appears to be the prominent leader at Jerusalem. He is mentioned several times in association with Peter.

With this insight, let us return to events that transpired in the life of Peter, as a disciple of our Lord. We begin by discovering where Jesus and his disciples traveled when they left the temple in Jerusalem.

Chapter Fourteen

PETER FOLLOWED JESUS IN JUDEA

TIME FRAME OF RECENT EVENTS
(John 3: 16, 22; 4: 2, 4-22, 27; Acts 10: 34-43)

Together, let us determine the time frame of recent events in our Lord's formal ministry. To assist us, we use the words of Elder McConkie regarding J. Reuben Clark, Jr. (See Note 1, end of chapter), who was a counselor to President David O. McKay, the ninth President of the Church in this dispensation: "President J. Reuben Clark, Jr.—than whom the Church has produced no greater scholar on all matters pertaining to the life of our Lord—has written a small booklet, less than one hundred pages, *Wist Ye Not That I Must Be About My Father's Business*, in which he traces Jesus' steps from Nazareth to Jerusalem . . . ."[89]

Later in his work, our apostolic scholar says, "Our friend and Brother, the Lord Jesus—and blessed be he—has now spent about two months in his active and formal ministry among men. As nearly as we can tell—and this is the chronology followed by President J. Reuben Clark, Jr.—Jesus was baptized by John in Jordan in January, A.D. 27; his forty days of fasting, prayer, and worship in the wilderness were in January and February (possibly continuing into March); probably he began to teach and call disciples (Andrew, Simon, and others) in February, not later than in March; and in March in Cana came the first public miracle, the changing of water into wine. Now it is Passover time, April 11-18, and the place is Jerusalem, the Holy City."[90]

With a different point of view, Elder Talmage says: "According to Luke (3: 23) Jesus was about thirty years of age at the time of His baptism, and we find that soon thereafter, He entered publicly upon the work of His ministry" (See *Jesus the Christ*, p. 166).

Therefore, from what Luke wrote, it appears evident that the correct year would be A.D. 30, instead of A.D. 27. The reader is informed that this work will continue to use the time frame used by Elder McConkie, but taking exception to the year.

The Passover mentioned—the first of four during our Lord's mortal ministry—had passed. During this time, our Lord had cleared the temple, foretold of his own death and resurrection, and taught Nicodemus the importance of the saving ordinances of the gospel. Now, Jesus and his disciples were in a place called Judea. Peter and his fellow disciples willingly followed Jesus to this area. None of them were compelled to stay with our Lord. As John (who was one of the disciples) has beautifully penned, each believed that "God so loved the world, that he gave his only begotten Son, that whosoever believed in him should not perish, but have everlasting life."

With this understanding, Elder Talmage explains: "Leaving Jerusalem, Jesus and His disciples went into the rural parts of Judea, and there tarried, doubtless preaching as opportunity was found or made; and those who believed on Him were baptized."[91] Using the time frame of President Clark, Elder McConkie asks and answers his own question: "For how long? For nine full months, . . . at which time—having, as Peter expressed it, preached 'throughout all Judea' that 'word which God sent unto the children of Israel'—he and his disciples went through Samaria (where the conversation at Jacob's Well took place) and into Galilee."[92]

The conversation between Jesus and the woman of Samaria undoubtedly was told to John and his fellow disciples by our Lord. We know this to be so, for John has written, "(For his disciples were gone away unto the city to buy meat.)" (Note: parentheses are with the scripture.) At the conclusion of the conversation, we read these words: "And upon this came his disciples, and marvelled that he talked with the woman: yet no man said, What seekest thou? Or, Why talkest thou with her?"

Regarding this early Judean ministry, we again learn from John that "Jesus and his disciples"—who, during this nine month period, we can safely believe included more than Peter, Andrew, James, John, Philip, and Nathanael; perhaps women were also traveling with them—tarried and baptized in the land of Judea.

JOHN THE BAPTIST, JESUS, AND PETER, MINISTERED IN JUDEA
(John 3: 22-23; Matt. 3: 16; Mark 1: 10)

It is important to note that John the Baptist, Jesus, Peter, and the other disciples, ministered in Judea at the same time. In addition, each taught the same gospel message—the same gospel that was revealed to the Prophet Joseph Smith in our day and time. With this knowledge, we turn our attention to John the Baptist. We read that, "John also was baptizing in Aenon near Salim, because there was much water there." If baptisms were performed by the mode of sprinkling only, there would be no need for "much water." Baptisms were performed by immersion, as was the case when John baptized our Lord. As Matthew and Mark have written, "And Jesus, when he was baptized, went up straightway out of the water . . . ."

THE DISCIPLES OF JOHN THE BAPTIST
(John 3: 24-36; Matt. 15: 1-20; Mark 7: 1-8, 19; Acts 10)

We read that "John was not yet cast into prison." "Then there arose a question between some of John's disciples and the Jews about purifying." According to apostate Jewish beliefs, the purifying power of baptism was an ordinance only needed for Gentile converts. Those individuals who were of the lineage of Abraham claimed they needed no baptism, only the cleansing ordinances that were established, such as the washing of hands before eating, and only eating certain meats.

From Elder Talmage, we read what transpired next: "With excusable ardor and well-intended zeal for their master, the disciples of John, who had been embroiled in the dispute, came to him saying, 'Rabbi, he [Jesus] that was with thee beyond Jordan, to whom thou barest witness, behold, the same baptizeth, and all men come to him.' John's supporters were concerned at the success of One whom they regarded in some measure as a rival to their beloved teacher."[93]

"And in the noble answer to it," as Farrar has admirably written, "all John's inherent greatness shown forth. He could not enter into rivalries, which would be a treachery against his deepest convictions, a falsification of his most solemn words. God was the sole source of human gifts, and in His sight there can be no such thing as human greatness. He reminded them... that he was *not* the Christ, but only his messenger; he was not the bridegroom, but the bridegroom's friend, and his heart was even now being gladdened by the bridegroom's voice. Henceforth he was content to decrease; content that his little light should be swallowed up in the boundless dawn. He was but an earthly messenger; but he had put the seal of his most intense conviction to the belief that God was true, and had given all things to His Son, and that through Him alone could eternal life be won"[94] (italics in quotation).

THE FATE OF JOHN THE BAPTIST
(Matt. 14: 3-12)

As to the future fate of John the Baptist, Elder Talmage states: "He had entered upon his work when sent of God so to do; he realized that his work had been in measure superseded, and he patiently awaited his release, in the meantime continuing in the ministry, directing souls to his Master. The beginning of the end was near. He was soon seized and thrown into a dungeon; where, as will be shown, he was beheaded to sate the vengeance of a corrupt woman whose sins he had boldly denounced."[95]

Therefore, John the Baptist, Jesus, Peter, and other disciples, taught the same gospel. As was explained to Nicodemus by our Lord, the first principles and ordinances of the gospel include the following: That an individual must have "faith in Jesus Christ as the Son of God, through whom alone men may gain eternal life; the forsaking of sin by resolute turning away from the gross darkness of evil to the saving light of righteousness; the unqualified requirement of a new birth through baptism in water, and this of necessity by the mode of immersion, since otherwise the figure of a birth would be meaningless; and the completion of the new birth through baptism by the Spirit—all these principles are taught herein in such simplicity and plainness as to make plausible no man's excuse for ignorance."

The gospel includes more—much more—than what was taught Nicodemus. The purpose of this work is not to expound or explain all of the doctrines of the gospel. Suffice it to say that

Peter and his fellow apostles taught the saving truths of the fullness of the gospel of Jesus Christ.

WERE PETER AND HIS FELLOW DISCIPLES BAPTIZED?
(Matt. 3: 13-16; John 3: 1-15)

Because John the Baptist baptized Jesus "to fulfill all right-eousness," and Jesus taught Nicodemus the doctrine that an individual must be "born of water and of the Spirit to enter into the kingdom of God," we can safely believe that Peter and his fellow disciples were baptized. Because Andrew and John were, at first, disciples of John the Baptist, we do not know if John baptized them. Because our Lord performed water baptisms, we may properly believe that Jesus personally baptized Peter and his fellow apostles.

PETER AND HIS FELLOW DISCIPLES
RECEIVED THE PRIESTHOOD

In addition to our Lord authorizing Peter and his fellow disciples to teach the gospel, we know that he gave them the priesthood. Whether Jesus ordained them elders in the Melchizedek Priesthood, or priests in the Aaronic Priesthood, we are not informed. Either office in the priesthood allows a person authority to baptize (See D&C 84: 26-30; 107: 1-14). To support the belief that the disciples had the priesthood, we read these informative words of Elder McConkie: "But at this time, in the early days of his early Judean ministry, Jesus and his disciples performed the same baptismal ordinance that John the Baptist was still performing. One of the things this means is that Jesus had already conferred the priesthood upon his newly-called disciples."[96]

In addition to John the Baptist baptizing those individuals who believed the gospel message, the Lord, himself, along with

Peter and his fellow disciples, were also baptizing converts. The following is derived from two sources: John the disciple, and the Joseph Smith Translation of the Bible.

JESUS AND HIS DISCIPLES PERFORMED
WATER BAPTISMS
(John 4: 1-3; JST 4: 2-4)

John the disciple says: "When therefore the Lord knew how the Pharisees had heard that Jesus made and baptized more disciples than John, (Though Jesus himself baptized not, but his disciples,) He left Judea, and departed again into Galilee."

However, from the Joseph Smith Translation of John, we learn this truth about Jesus: "They sought more diligently some means that they might put him to death; for many received John as a prophet, but they believed not on Jesus. Now the Lord knew this, though he himself baptized not so many as his disciples; For he suffered them for an example, preferring one another."

"Contrary to the false teachings and traditions of sectarianism," explains Elder McConkie, "Jesus personally performed water baptisms so that in all things he might be the great Exemplar. Without question he also performed all other ordinances essential to salvation and exaltation."[97]

THE MISSION OF THE DISCIPLES

As related earlier, Peter and his fellow disciples had traveled with Jesus for nine months. While following our Lord, these chosen men had learned and seen much. To explain, Elder McConkie has written: "Since then all of these brethren have been with Jesus in much of his ministry. They saw the water become wine, the moneychangers flee from the temple, the miracles wrought at the Passover and throughout all Judea. They know what Jesus said to Nicodemus and the woman of Samaria, nor is the episode involving the nobleman's son hidden from them. They were present or at least know what he said in the synagogue in Nazareth. By now they have spent hundreds, perhaps thousands, of hours conversing with and listening to the Master."[98]

For these many months Peter, Andrew, James, John, Philip and Nathanael willingly left their trades, and their families, and have followed our Lord to various celebrations and locations. However, they had not as yet been called into a full-time ministry. As Edersheim has explained: "From the character of the narrative [who was from John], and still more from their later call of these four [Peter, Andrew, James, and John], it would seem that, after the return of Jesus from Judea into Galilee, His disciples had left Him, probably in Cana, and returned to their homes and ordinary avocations. They were not yet called to forsake all and follow Him . . . ."[99]

NOTE

1. J. Reuben Clark, Jr. was sustained as Second Counselor to President Heber J. Grant on April 6, 1933, at age 61; sustained as First Counselor to President Grant on October 6, 1934; ordained an apostle on October 11, 1934, at age 63, by President Grant; sustained as First Counselor to President George Albert Smith on May 21, 1945; sustained as Second Counselor to President David O. McKay on April 9, 1951; sustained as First Counselor to President McKay on June 12, 1959. He died October 6, 1961, at Salt Lake City, Utah, at age 90.

Chapter Fifteen

PETER CALLED TO BE
A FISHER OF MEN

JESUS TRAVELED TOWARD CAPERNAUM
(John 4: 4-25, 46-54; Luke 4: 16-32)

After Peter and his fellow disciples left Jesus in or around Cana, our Lord continued to teach the gospel and perform miracles as he traveled to Capernaum in Galilee. He taught the woman of Samaria that the "living waters" of the gospel lead to eternal life. Without meeting the child, Jesus healed the son of a nobleman. Our Lord's Messianic claims were rejected in Nazareth, the city "where he had been brought up."

ON THE SHORE OF THE SEA OF GALILEE
(Matt. 14: 34; Mark 6: 53; Luke 5: 1; John 1: 23; 21: 1; Numb. 34: 11; Josh. 12: 3; Josh. 19: 35)

Now, early in the morning, Jesus walked on the shore of the Sea of Galilee near Capernaum. Regarding this body of water, Elder Talmage explains: "This, the largest body of fresh water in Palestine, is somewhat pear-shape in outline and measures approximately thirteen miles in extreme length on a northerly-southerly line and between six and seven miles in greatest width . . . . Adjoining the lake on the northwest is a plain, which in earlier times was highly cultivated: this was known as the land of Gennesaret; and the water body came to be known as the sea or lake of Gennesaret. From the prominence of one of the cities on its western shore, it was known also as the Sea of Tiberias. In the Old Testament it is called the Sea of Chinnereth or Chinneroth after the name of a contiguous [nearby] city."[100]

PETER AND ANDREW WERE CALLED
TO FOLLOW JESUS
(Matt. 4: 18-20; Mark 1: 16-18)

Let us picture the following scene: Near the shore, "Simon called Peter, and Andrew his brother" were in their commercial fishing boat "casting a net into the sea: for they were fishers." To help us realize the significance of this event, we use the words of Edersheim: "Engaged in their fishing on the afternoon, evening, and night of [Jesus'] arrival in Capernaum, they would probably not have known His presence till He spake to them. But he had come that morning specially to seek four of these fishers, that He might, now that the time for it had come, call them to permanent discipleship—and, what is more, fit them for the work to which He would call them."[101]

Then, Peter and his brother, Andrew, heard that familiar and friendly voice of our Lord calling them to "permanent discipleship" by these stirring words of invitation: "Follow me, and I will make you fishers of men." It is reasonable to believe that Jesus said more—much more—to these believing and faithful brothers than what is briefly written by Matthew and Mark. All that we know is that Peter and Andrew, because of their total love and devotion for our Lord, "left their nets, and followed him."

JAMES AND JOHN WERE CALLED
TO FOLLOW JESUS
(Matt. 4: 21-22; Mark 1: 19-20)

Let us visualize what transpired next: Though the scriptural record does not mention them being present, by reason that Peter and Andrew "left their nets, and followed [Jesus]," we may safely suppose they were present when the next call was extended. Walking farther along the shoreline, Jesus saw "James the son of Zebedee, and John his brother, in a ship with Zebedee their father, mending their nets; and he called them." As with Peter and Andrew, we do not fully know what our Lord said to James and John. Whatever was spoken, and because of their total love and devotion for our Lord, we read "and they left their father Zebedee in the ship with the hired servants, and went after him."

THE ACCOUNT WRITTEN BY LUKE
(Luke 4: 38-39; 5: 1-11)

We now turn our attention to the account written by Luke. Whether this event happened in conjunction with the calls given to the two sets of brothers or occurred shortly thereafter, we are not fully informed. Farrar writes that this call transpired after Jesus had healed the fever that was afflicting Peter's mother-in-law.[102] However, in writing of the events that transpired in the life of our Lord, Alfred Edersheim and Elders Talmage and McConkie each write that it transpired before Peter's mother-in-law was healed.[103] According to Luke's gospel, Farrar is correct in his statement. No matter when this event transpired, let us consider the significance of the call to the two sets of brothers.

JESUS ENTERED SIMON PETER'S SHIP
(Luke 5: 1-10)

The fame of our Lord had spread throughout Galilee. Standing on the shore of the Sea of Galilee, a large crowd of people "pressed upon him" so they could "hear the word of God." Jesus saw two boats anchored by the "lake" and the owners were on shore "washing their nets."

Our Lord "entered into one of the ships, which was Simon's" and asked him "that he would thrust out a little from the land. And he sat down, and taught the people out of the ship." Obediently, Peter moved his boat away from the shore.

It is interesting to note Edersheim, Farrar, and Elder Talmage each used the same word to describe the ship Jesus preached in. Edersheim wrote these words: "The boat of Peter shall be His pulpit."[104] Farrar has written: "Seated in this pleasant pulpit, safe from the inconvenient contact with the multitude."[105] Elder Talmage penned these words: "Seating Himself, as teachers of that time usually did in delivering discourses, the Lord preached from this floating pulpit to the multitude on shore. The subject of the address is not given us."[106]

When our Lord finished teaching the people, "he said unto Simon, Launch out into the deep, and let down your nets for a draught."

PETER WAS SUBMISSIVE AND OBEDIENT

To better understand the character of Peter, we listen to his response to Jesus. Not in the spirit of doubt, but only giving explanation, Simon Peter respectfully answered, "Master, we have toiled all the night, and have taken nothing." To demonstrate his submissive and obedient nature, he quickly replied, "nevertheless at thy word I will let down the net." When the nets were lowered, he and his fishing partners caught "a great multitude of fishes: and their net brake" (the footnote wording: "or was breaking").

To clarify the meaning of this miracle, Edersheim says: "The 'nevertheless, at Thy word,' marks the new trust, and the new work as springing from that trust . . . . But what did it mean to Simon Peter? He had been called to full discipleship, and he had obeyed the call. He had been in his boat beside the Saviour, and heard what He had spoken, and it had gone to his heart . . . The miraculous was, that the Lord had seen through those waters down where the multitude of fishes was, and bidden him let down for a draught. He could see through the intervening waters, right down to the bottom of that sea."[107]

"DEPART FROM ME"
(Luke 5: 10)

From Luke, we read what transpired next: "And they [Peter and Andrew] beckoned unto their partners [James and John], which were in the other ship, that they should come and help them. And they came, and filled both the ships, so that they began to sink. When Simon Peter saw [the miracle of fishes], he fell down at Jesus' knees, saying, Depart from me; for I am a sinful man, O Lord."

From Farrar, we learn what Peter said to our Lord: "St. Peter did not *mean* the 'Depart from me;' he only meant—and this was known to the Searcher of hearts—'I am utterly unworthy to be near Thee, yet let me stay'"[108] (italics in quotation).

Those individuals who have been in the presence of one of the Lord's anointed servants, and especially a prophet of God, in some measure, can appreciate how Peter felt at this time on the boat. Though this senior disciple had traveled with Jesus for several months, and had a burning testimony that he was the Messiah, after seeing the miracle of fishes, Peter, at that particular moment, felt unworthy to be in the presence of one so great and righteous—the God of heaven and earth.

In addition to this, it is important to know that this was no ordinary experience of catching fish for Peter and his partners. Over the years, these fishing partners had caught many fish in their nets. Having been successful in their trade, they had become wealthy. Peter, Andrew, James, and John, along with hired servants, had toiled all the night and caught nothing. Then, at the word of Jesus, they caught "a great multitude of fishes," and their nets were breaking. Further, they "filled both the ships, so that they began to sink." This amount of fish was more than they had ever caught previously in one catch. To understand their surprise and wonderment, Luke wrote that Peter "was astonished, and all that were with him, at the draught of the fishes which they had taken: And so was also James, and John, the sons of Zebedee, which were partners with Simon."

We learn what Jesus said to the disciples by what Farrar wrote: "And how gently the answer came: 'Fear not; from henceforth thou shalt catch men.'"[109]

Immediately these words comforted and inspired Peter. In addition, this marvelous promise changed his life, and those of his partners.

PETER AND HIS FELLOW DISCIPLES FOLLOWED JESUS
(Luke 5: 11)

Regarding Peter's submissive and obedient nature, and those of his partners, we read that they "brought their ships to land, [and] they forsook all, and followed him." We may properly wonder what Peter said to his family regarding his call to "permanent discipleship." We know that Peter was a devoted and dedicated person, or else he would not have followed Jesus for nine months. Therefore, we can properly believe that he was equally dedicated and devoted to his family. Because his family knew of his conversion, and they, themselves, believed that Jesus was the Christ, we can be assured that Peter's family supported his decision of being a permanent disciple of our Lord. With this understanding, we turn our attention to events that transpired in or near Simon Peter's home in Capernaum.

Chapter Sixteen

EVENTS IN OR NEAR PETER'S HOME

PETER'S MOTHER-IN-LAW HEALED BY JESUS
(Mark 1: 21-31; Luke 4: 31-39; Matt. 8: 14-15)

It was a Sabbath day in Capernaum. Peter and his fellow disciples went to the synagogue to listen to Jesus teach the gospel. While teaching, the people in the congregation "were astonished at his doctrine: for he taught them as one that had authority." In this place, our Lord cast out an evil spirit, and those in attendance "were all amazed."

Following the synagogue service, Peter and Andrew, in company with Jesus, walked toward Simon Peter's home. James and John were also invited guests. As was the custom of the day, a festive Sabbath meal was enjoyed at family gatherings. Sabbath feasts were the most joyous occasions of the week. However, upon entering Simon's house, no festive meal awaited them, only the news that "Simon's wife's mother lay sick of a fever."

Regarding this illness afflicting Peter's mother-in-law, Edersheim says: "From the Synagogue we follow the Saviour, in company with His called disciples, to Peter's wedded home. But no festive meal, as was Jewish wont, awaited them there. A sudden access of violent 'burning fever,' . . . had laid Peter's mother-in-law prostrate."[110]

Farrar says, "Rising from the seat . . . in the synagogue,

Christ retired into the house of Simon . . . and his wife's mother lay stricken down by a violent access of fever."¹¹¹

Luke has written that this woman was afflicted with "a great fever."

Whatever caused this "fever," Simon's mother-in-law was not well. Being compassionate, we see Peter, along with his wife, asking Jesus to give her a blessing of health. For as Luke has written: "and they besought him for her." Mark says: "and anon [immediately] they tell him of her." Peter's home was a household of faith. Therefore, it was natural and proper for Peter and his wife to ask Jesus, who was the great "Healer," to heal a loved one.

Regarding the process of healing Peter's mother-in-law, Matthew wrote that Jesus "touched her hand, and the fever left her." Mark has written that our Lord "took her by the hand, and lifted her up; and immediately the fever left her." Luke explains that Christ "stood over her, and rebuked the fever; and it left her: and immediately she arose and ministered unto them." Combining the words of the gospel writers, we can picture the following scene: Jesus stood over her, or beside her, verbally rebuked the illness, and touched her hand by taking it in his hand, and physically "lifted her up," out of bed. "Immediately the fever left her, and she ministered unto them."

After this healing, we wonder what words of thanks and praise were expressed to our Lord. Whatever was spoken, we know that the members of Peter's family were very thankful. Nourishment was derived from eating fish, bread, and drink, prepared by the woman whose body but moments earlier was afflicted with a great fever. Truly this was a festive Sabbath meal. All who were in attendance were blessed both physically and spiritually.

HEALINGS IN FRONT OF PETER'S HOME
(Mark 1: 3, 35; Matt 8: 16; Luke 4: 40; Acts 3: 1-8; Luke 4: 42)

This was not all that transpired at Peter's home that memorable day. As Edersheim states: "It was evening. The sun was setting, and the Sabbath past. All that day it had been told from home to home what had been done in the Synagogue; it had been whispered what had taken place in the house of their neighbour [sic] Simon."[112]

The word rapidly spread through Capernaum that Jesus had the power to cast out devils and heal those who were ill. People with all kinds of afflictions began gathering in front of Simon Peter's home. For as Mark explains: "And at even, when the sun did set, they brought unto him all that were diseased, and them that were possessed with devils. And all the city was gathered together at the door."

Matthew has written: "When the even was come, they brought unto him many that were possessed with devils: and he cast out the spirits with his word, and healed all that were sick."

Without either touching or seeing individuals, Jesus had healed many people in the past. Now, to help increase the faith of those who had came to Peter's door, Jesus walked out of the house and as Luke says, "and he laid his hands on every one of them, and healed them. And devils also came out of many, crying out, and saying, Thou art Christ the Son of God. And he rebuking them suffered them not to speak: for they knew that he was Christ."

Imagine how this display of compassion and healing affected Peter's emotions and thoughts, and those of his fellow disciples. In later years, when a lame man from birth asked financial help from Peter and John, as "they went up together into the temple," Peter had compassion for the sufferer. Just as Peter's mother-in-law had been lifted up out of her bed of affliction by the hand of Jesus, so also Peter took the man "by the right hand, and lifted him up: and immediately his feet and ankle bones received strength. And he leaping up stood, and walked, and entered with them into the temple, walking, and leaping, and praising God."

Returning to the Sabbath day narrative, this truly was a marvelous day of preaching and healing. Truly, this was a day of learning and rejoicing. Now, after the healings had ended, those individuals who were staying in Peter's home retired to bed to receive needed sleep. Then, "in the morning, rising up a great while before day, [Jesus] went out, and departed into a solitary place, and there prayed."

SIMON PETER AND OTHERS FOUND JESUS
(Mark 1: 36-38; Luke 4: 42-43)

Evidently, Peter and his fellow disciples knew where our Lord had gone to pray, for as Mark explains, "And Simon and they that were with him followed after him. And when they had found him, they said unto him, All men seek for thee." Soon the multitude gathered about him and pleaded that he stay with them in Capernaum. Luke also states, ". . . the people sought him, and came unto him, and stayed with him, that he should not depart from them."

With kindness, our Lord told the people, "I must preach the kingdom of God to other cities also: for therefore am I sent." Then, to his "permanent disciples," he stated, "Let us go into the next towns, that I may preach there also: for therefore came I forth."

Elder McConkie has written these brief but informative words concerning Jesus, Peter and his fellow disciples: "And

preach [the gospel] he did, in Galilee (except for a brief attendance at his second Passover), for almost two years, for about
twenty-one months. By then it will be October 29, and he will
go to the Feast of Tabernacles to commence his later Judean
ministry. But now he is starting his first tour of Galilee,
preaching, healing, doing good, and working righteousness."[113]

BACK AT PETER'S HOME
(Mark 1: 28; 2: 1-12; Luke 4: 37; 5: 17-24; Matt. 9: 2-8)

Following this second Galilean tour of healing the sick,
casting out devils, and teaching the gospel, both Peter and
Jesus were back in Capernaum. As was his practice, our Lord
stayed in the home of Peter, who was recognized as the
presiding disciple. As Edersheim has written: "For, no sooner
'was it heard that He was in the house,' or, as some have
rendered it, 'that He was at home,' than so many flocked to the
dwelling of Peter, which at that period may have been 'the
house' or temporary 'home' of the Saviour . . . ."[114]

In Peter's home, Christ was among friends and believers.
While there, our Lord received needed rest, nourishment, and
sociability. Even before going to Capernaum, the fame of Jesus
was known throughout Palestine. From what transpired about
twenty-one months previously, in front of Simon's home, the
people in this town were anxious to be with Jesus. Considering
what transpired, Elder Talmage says: "His place of abode in
Capernaum was well known, and word was soon noised about
that He was in the house. A great throng gathered, so that there
was no room to receive them; even the doorway was crowded,
and later comers could not get near the Master. To all who were
within hearing Jesus preached the gospel."[115]

Peter must have had a large home. Every room was full of
people who were desirous of hearing and seeing Jesus.

Describing who was in attendance "in the house," we again use the words of Elder Talmage: "Among the people there assembled were scribes, Pharisees, and doctors of the law, not only representatives of the local synagog but some who had come from distant towns in Galilee, and some from Judea, and even from Jerusalem. The official class had opposed our Lord and His works on earlier occasions, and their presence in the house at this time boded further unfriendly criticism and possible obstruction."[116]

IN PETER'S HOME,
JESUS HEALED A MAN WITH PALSY
(Matt. 3: 3; 9: 2-7; Mark 2: 3-14; Luke 5: 19-26)

While Jesus was teaching in Peter's home, four men brought a man who was afflicted with Palsy, which rendered him helpless. So desirous were they of seeing the Savior, they broke through the roof of Peter's house and lowered the man on his bed into the room where our Lord was teaching. As Mark has written, "When Jesus saw their faith, he said unto the sick of the palsy, Son, thy sins be forgiven thee." The scribes who were in attendance reasoned in their hearts, "Why doth this man thus speak blasphemies? Who can forgive sins but God only?" Jesus perceived their thoughts and said to them, "Why reason ye these things in your hearts? Whether is it easier to say to the sick of the palsy, Thy sins be forgiven thee; or to say, Arise, and take up thy bed, and walk?" Proclaiming to all who were present who he was, our Lord boldly declared, "But that ye may know that the Son of man hath power on earth to forgive sins, (he saith to the sick of palsy,) I say unto thee, Arise, and take up thy bed, and go thy way into thine house."

Then, "immediately he arose, took up the bed, and went forth before them all; insomuch that they were all amazed and glorified God."

Following this healing, Jesus left Peter's home and the people followed him by the seaside. Jesus saw Matthew, who is also known as Levi, and called him to be a disciple.

PREPARATION OF PETER
(Acts 4: 6-13)

From what transpired in his home, Peter observed that no matter who was in attendance, our Savior taught the gospel "as one that had authority." Peter also observed that in the face of opposition, Jesus was neither timid nor afraid to speak the truth, and that when faith was exercised, our Lord blessed and healed the afflicted individual.

To demonstrate that Peter typified our Lord, we turn once again to the account written in Acts, when this senior apostle was arrested. In front of "Annas the high priest, and Caiaphas, and John, and Alexander, and as many as were of the kindred of the high priest, were gathered together at Jerusalem. And when they had set [Peter and John] in the midst, they asked, By what Power, or by what name, have ye done this [healed the man at the temple gate]?

"Then Peter, filled with the Holy Ghost," spoke these stirring words: "Ye rulers of the people, and elders of Israel. If we this day be examined of the good deed done to the impotent man, by what means he is made whole; Be it known unto you all, and to all the people of Israel, that by the name of Jesus Christ of Nazareth, whom ye crucified, whom God raised from the dead, even by him doth this man stand here before you whole. This is the stone which was set at [naught] of you builders, which is become the head of the corner. Neither is there salvation in any other: for there is none other name under heaven given among men, whereby we must be saved.

"Now when they saw the boldness of Peter and John, and perceived that they were unlearned and ignorant men, they marveled; and they took knowledge of them, and they had been with Jesus."

After "beholding the man which was healed standing with them, they could say nothing against it." After conferring, the council "commanded them not to speak at all nor teach in the name of Jesus."

Courageously, Peter and John answered and said unto them: "Whether it be right in the sight of God to hearken unto you more than unto God, judge ye. For we cannot but speak the things which we have seen and heard."

Therefore, the council "let them go, finding nothing how they might punish them."

From the day that Andrew brought Simon Peter to meet the Messiah, our Savior was preparing and training his senior disciple for the high and holy calling that was forthcoming.

Chapter Seventeen

PETER WAS CALLED TO BE THE SENIOR APOSTLE

THE CALLING OF THE TWELVE
(D&C 107: 23, 33; 1 Cor. 12: 28; Eph. 4:11-15)

From Elder McConkie, we gather the following information: "Jesus is now going to call the Twelve: twelve men who will be his witnesses; who will bear, with him, the burdens of the kingdom; who will accept martyrdom and defy the rulers of the world; and who, save Judas Iscariot and John the Beloved, shall seal their testimonies with their own blood."

". . . It is the summer of A.D. 28 [From Luke: A.D. 31], in less than two years (April of A.D. 30) [From Luke: A.D. 33] he (Jesus) will finish his mortal labors, ascend unto his Father, and leave the Twelve to preach the gospel in all the world and to build up that church and kingdom which will administer salvation to all who believe and obey."[117]

The glorious day finally arrived for establishing the foundation of The Church of Jesus Christ—which Church was and.is the Kingdom of God on earth. To help people identify the true church of Christ, Paul, who was an apostle, has written the following information: "And God hath set some in the church, *first apostles*, secondarily prophets, thirdly teachers." Then, the following are given to bless and strengthen the organization: "after that miracles, then gifts of healings, helps, governments, diversities of tongues" (italics added).

To make clear why our Lord established his Church with various officers in the organization, we rely again upon Paul for understanding: "And he gave some, apostles; and some, prophets; and some evangelists; and some, pastors and teachers; For the perfecting of the saints, for the work of the ministry, for the edifying of the body of Christ: Till we all come in the unity of the faith, and of the knowledge of the Son of God, unto a perfect man, unto the measure of the stature of the fulness of Christ. That we henceforth be no more children, tossed to and fro, and carried about with every wind of doctrine, by the sleight of men, and cunning craftiness, whereby they lie in wait to deceive."

Therefore, the true Church of Jesus Christ will have apostles, prophets, and teachers, all of whom are called of God and endowed with power to "regulate all the affairs of the same in all nations." And where none of these officers are found in the Church, the Kingdom of God is not established on the earth. Therefore, these servants "speaking the truth in love," guide and direct the Lord's Church on earth.

INFORMATION REGARDING THE TWELVE
(Abr. 3: 22-23; 1 Ne. 1: 9-10; 12: 8-10; Mormon 3: 19; Rev. 21: 10-14; D&C 29: 12)

Among the "noble and great ones," as seen by Abraham, the Twelve Apostles were chosen, before they were born, to be rulers in Christ's Church. They were foreordained to come in the meridian of time, to serve as special witnesses of our Lord and Savior.

Six hundred years before the birth of Christ, Lehi saw the Twelve Apostles in vision. Nephi, who was the son of Lehi, wrote these informative words: "And it came to pass that he saw One descending out of the midst of heaven, and he beheld that his luster was above that of the sun at noon-day. And he also saw twelve others following him, and their brightness did exceed that of the stars in the firmament."

When the Nephite Twelve were chosen, our Lord gave them the same authority as he gave the Jewish Twelve. From Nephi and Mormon, we read the following information about the two sets of Twelve Apostles: "And I write also unto the remnant of this people, who shall also be judged by the twelve whom Jesus chose in this land; and they shall be judged by the other twelve whom Jesus chose in the land of Jerusalem. And these things doth the Spirit manifest unto me; therefore I write unto you all."

Because there are twelve tribes in Israel, so there are Twelve Apostles who preside over Israel and the world. Regarding Jerusalem, in its celestial glory, John the Revelator saw it "descending out of heaven from God." This city "had a wall great and high, and [it] had twelve gates," and on these gates, "are the names of the twelve tribes of the children of Israel." And, "the wall of the city had twelve foundations, and [on] them [were written] the names of the Twelve Apostles of the Lamb."

John the Revelator saw the Jewish Twelve, who will preside over the Nephite Twelve, as well as Latter-day Twelve, in our dispensation. Excepting Judas Iscariot, all who are called to serve in the Quorum of the Twelve Apostles "are righteous forever; for because of their faith in the Lamb of God their garments are made white in his blood."

In addition, the Lord has revealed the following informa-tion about the second coming of Christ: "And again, verily, verily, I say unto you, and it hath gone forth in a firm decree, by the will of the Father, that mine apostles, the Twelve, which were with me in my ministry at Jerusalem, shall stand at my right hand at the day of my coming in a pillar of fire, being clothed with robes of righteousness, with crowns upon their heads, in glory even as I am, to judge the whole house of Israel, even as many as have loved me and kept my commandments, and none else."

JESUS PRAYED TO KNOW THE TWELVE
(Luke 6: 13)

A day before our Lord called the Jewish Twelve, he "went out into a mountain to pray, and continued all night in prayer to God." It is worth noting that Jesus spent a night in prayer asking his Father in Heaven who should be chosen to be his Twelve Apostles. Throughout the New Testament, we observe that Jesus prayed often to his Father. Accordingly, his fervent prayers demonstrated his great humility and acknowledgement of the Giver of all blessings.

Then, "when it was day, he called unto him his disciples: and of them he chose twelve, whom also he named apostles."

PETER BECAME THE SENIOR APOSTLE
(Matt. 10: 2-4; Mark 3: 13-21; Luke 6: 12-16; John 15: 15-16)

Regarding Peter being the senior member of the Twelve, Elder Talmage states: "The three Gospel-writers who make record of the organization of the Twelve place Simon Peter first and Judas Iscariot last in the category; they agree also in the relative position of some but not of all the others. Following the order given by Mark, and this may be the most convenient since he names as the first three those who later became most prominent, we have the following list: Simon Peter, James (son of Zebedee), John (brother of the last-named), Andrew (brother of Simon Peter), Philip, Bartholomew (or Nathanael), Matthew, Thomas, James (son of Alpheus), Judas (also known as Lebbeus or Thaddeus), Simon (distinguished by his surname Zelotes, also known as the Canaanite), and Judas Iscariot."[118]

Imagine how Peter must have felt being honored with this call to be the senior apostle of our Lord. When first introduced to the Messiah by his brother Andrew, our Lord bestowed upon him a new name, which designated him a seer. Probably in February of A.D. 27 [From Luke: A.D. 30], Jesus called him to be a disciple. Then, this noble man received another call to be a "permanent disciple." Obediently and submissively, Peter followed our Lord to various celebrations and locations. He willing left his fishing business and his family to serve the Lord. Now, in the summer of A.D. 28 [From Luke: A.D. 31], he was called to be the senior apostle. In approximately two years, Peter would become the President of the Church, following the crucifixion of Jesus. For the present, this great man would be tutored and molded for the leadership role that he would assume.

The Savior explained to Peter and those who were chosen to serve with him in the Quorum of the Twelve: "Henceforth I call you not servants; for the servant knoweth not what his lord doeth; but I have called you friends; for all things that I have heard of my Father I have made known unto you. You have not chosen me, but I have chosen you, and ordained you, that ye should go and bring forth fruit, and that your fruit should remain; that whatsoever ye shall ask of the Father in my name, he may give it you."

Accordingly, Peter and his fellow apostles became "special witnesses of the name of Christ in all the world." In the near future, they would be "set apart as members of the Quorum of the Twelve and . . . given the keys and power to preside over the church and kingdom and regulate all of the affairs of God on earth. In addition, they would be "a Traveling Presiding High

Council, to officiate in the name of the Lord, . . . to build up the church, and regulate all the affairs of the same in all nations, first unto the Gentiles and secondly unto the Jews" (D&C 107:33).

Now that Peter was called to be the senior apostle, we will observe him in different settings. Let us turn our attention to a display of Peter's faith; a faith so great that it has never been duplicated—as far as has been recorded—by another mortal man, excepting our Lord.

Chapter Eighteen

PETER WALKED ON THE SEA
OF GALILEE

PETER AND HIS FELLOW APOSTLES WERE
GIVEN POWER AND AUTHORITY
(Matt. 10: 1, 5-33; Mark 6: 7-13; Luke 6: 40; 9: 1-6; 12: 1-12;
Acts 3: 1-8; 9: 36-42)

Preparatory to understanding what happened on the Sea of Galilee, we must first learn what transpired in Peter's life after he was called to be the senior apostle. Our Lord sent him, along with his fellow members of the Twelve, on missions, traveling two by two, without purse or provisions, to the cities and villages of Palestine. In addition, he gave these chosen men instructions and commandments to help them in their apostolic ministry.

Prior to being sent on their missions, our Lord called his Twelve disciples together, and gave them power and authority. What power and authority were given to Peter and his fellow apostles? He gave them the priesthood, which allowed them to act in his name, to teach the gospel, perform baptisms by immersion, cast out evil spirits, "and to heal all manner of sickness and all manner of disease." In addition, he also gave them the power to raise the dead.

Signs always follow faith, and miracles always attend faith. Truly, faith precedes the miracle. Faith allows the sick to be healed, devils to be cast out, and the dead brought back to life.

Because of his apostolic calling, Peter performed each of these priesthood ordinances while serving his brief mission of probably three months. Then, while serving as the President of the Church, Simon Peter—by the priesthood and by the power of faith—preached the gospel, healed the sick, made a lame man whole, and most prominently, restored life to a deceased woman of Joppa, named Dorcas. With this understanding, we turn to events that led to Peter walking on the water.

PETER AND HIS FELLOW APOSTLES WERE
"CONSTRAINED" TO ENTER A SHIP
(Matt. 14: 13-23; Mark 6: 30-46; Luke 9: 10-17; John 6: 1-15)

From John's gospel, we learn that the Passover, "a feast of the Jews, was nigh." Mark's gospel informs us that the multitude, composed of five thousand men, in company with women and children, sat "upon the green grass." Therefore, according to the time frame we are using, it was springtime, probably early April of A.D. 29 [From Luke: A.D. 32]. This was the second Passover in the mortal ministry of Jesus.

After the multitude was miraculously fed with five loaves of bread and two small fishes, the people, in their enthusiasm, were going to take Jesus by force, and compel him to be their king. In order to keep Peter and his fellow apostles from being involved with this unrighteous plan, we read, "And Jesus constrained his disciples to get into a ship, and go before him unto the other side."

Regarding sending the apostles into the boat, we turn to Elder Talmage for understanding: "The disciples hesitated to leave their Master; but He constrained them and they obeyed. His insistence that the Twelve depart from both Himself and the multitude, may have been due to a desire to protect the chosen disciples against possible infection by the materialistic and unrighteous designs of the throng to make Him King. By means that are not detailed, He caused the people to disperse; and, as night came on, He found that for which He had come in quest, solitude and quiet. Ascending the hill, He chose a secluded place, and there remained in prayer during the greater part of the night."[119]

THE STORM ON THE SEA OF GALILEE
(Matt. 14: 22-33; Mark 6: 45-52; John 6: 5-6, 15-21)

Together, let us discover what transpired in the life of Peter and his fellow apostles after they entered the ship. They began to sail toward Bethsaida, which was four miles from Capernaum, and both cities shared a common harbor. Over the years, Peter and Andrew, as well as James and John, as fishing partners, had encountered many storms upon the Sea of Galilee. Suddenly, the soft night breeze increased into a fierce and violent wind. The ship was greatly tossed about in the surging waves. As Matthew has written: "The ship was now in the midst of the sea, tossed with waves: for the wind was contrary." Regarding our Lord watching his apostles being buffeted by the wind, Mark says: "And he saw them toiling in rowing; for the wind was contrary unto them."

We further discover that this storm happened "about the fourth watch of the night." Regarding this watch, we rely again upon Elder Talmage for understanding: "During the greater part of the Old Testament time, the people of Israel divided the night into three watches, each of four hours, such a period being that of individual sentinel duty. Before the beginning of the Christian-era, however, the Jews had adopted the Roman order of four night-watches, each lasting three hours .... The fourth watch was the last of the three-hour periods between sunset and sunrise, or between 6 P.M. and 6 A.M. and therefore extended from 3 to 6 o'clock in the morning."[120]

So strong was the wind that those in the boat had only "rowed about five and twenty or thirty furlongs." A furlong is an eighth of a mile. Therefore, the vessel had only traveled about three and a half miles in eight or ten hours. According to Farrar, "the ship had traversed but half of its destined course."[121]

"IT IS I; BE NOT AFRAID"

The length and severity of the storm had intensified the concerns and fears of all the individuals who were on the boat. When the strength of the Twelve was nearly gone, our Lord came to their rescue. "Jesus went unto them," not by land, but by walking on the sea.

Even among the most righteous mortals, faith is enjoyed in varying degrees. Though a man lacks the faith to move a mountain, he has the faith to heal the sick. At that moment on the Sea of Galilee, Peter's faith was tested, along with his colleagues, when our Lord did not approach the ship directly but walked as if he "would have passed by them." "And when the disciples saw him walking on the sea, they were troubled," and they exclaimed, "It is a spirit." What else were these men to think? Never before had it been recorded that a mortal man walked upon the water. Besides toiling against the fierce wind and boisterous waves, the Twelve thought that they were encountering an added peril—an evil, tormenting spirit. Being human, "they cried out for fear."

Then, Jesus spoke those assuring and comforting words, "Be of good cheer; it is I; be not afraid." Immediately, Peter and his fellow apostles recognized the familiar voice of their beloved Lord and Master.

PETER WALKED ON THE WATER

Not fully understanding how faith works, some individuals have implied that Peter's request to walk upon the water demonstrated his impulsive nature. To illustrate, we use the words of Farrar: "That Voice stilled their terrors, and at once they were eager to receive Him into the ship; but Peter's impetuous love—the strong yearning of him who, in his despairing self-consciousness, had cried out 'Depart from me!' now cannot even await His approach, and he passionately exclaims: 'Lord, if it be Thou, bid me come unto Thee on the water.'"[122]

With another view, Edersheim has written the following explanation: "In order to understand the request of Peter: 'Lord, if it be Thou, bid me come to Thee on the water.' They are the words of a man, whom the excitement of the moment has carried beyond all reflection. And yet this combination of doubt ('if it be Thou'), with presumption ('bid me come on the water')—and hope is a combination of doubt and presumption, but also their transformation. With reverence be it said, Christ could not have left the request ungranted, even though it was the outcome of yet unreconciled and untransformed doubt and presumption."[123]

Using similar thoughts of Edersheim, Elder Talmage has written the following explanation: "It was on Peter's own request that he was permitted to attempt the feat. Had Jesus forbidden him, the man's faith might have suffered a check; his attempt, though attended by partial failure, was a demonstration of the efficacy of faith in the Lord, such as no verbal teaching could ever have conveyed."[124]

How does an individual rank the miracles performed by our Lord and his fellow servants? Which of these takes more faith: restoring life to a deceased person or walking on water? Both miracles require a tremendous amount of faith. As it pertains to Peter's faith on the Sea of Galilee, his miracle was great. As far as recorded, no other mortal man, excepting our Lord, has defied gravity and walked on water.

Now that Peter's faith was renewed, he was eager, ready to act, and he "said, Lord, if it be thou, bid me come unto thee on the water." There is not much faith expressed in the phrase: "if it be thou." Perhaps, this righteous man inadvertently used the word "if," when he should have used the word "as " or "since." No matter what word was spoken, our Lord knew what Peter was requesting. Above the boisterous wind, and unruly waves, the senior apostle asked in faith, "bid me come unto thee on the water." Granting permission, our Lord invited Peter to join him with this singular response, "Come."

Regarding faith, and applying it to Peter's faith, Elder McConkie states: "If there is faith, there will be miracles; if there are no miracles, there is no faith . . . . Faith and miracles go together, always and everlasting, and faith precedes the miracle. Faith is power, the power of God, the power by which the worlds were made. Where there is faith there is power . . . ."[125]

With this understanding, we witness a display of this senior apostle's faith; a faith so great that it has never been duplicated by another mortal man, excepting our Lord. Therefore, "when Peter was come down out of the ship, he walked on the water, to go to Jesus."

Being raised around the sea, Peter knew that it was impossible for a man to walk on water. Yet, when he was ordained to be the senior apostle, Jesus had given him the priesthood, which gave him the authority to act in Christ's name. Following the example of our Lord, Peter also performed water baptisms, healed the sick, cast out evil spirits, raised the dead, and was eventually crucified on a cross.

Now, on the Sea of Galilee, Peter was only following the example of Jesus, the Master Teacher. Truly, faith precedes the miracle. Because Peter walked on the water, it verifies, for that particular moment, he had the same faith and power as our Lord to walk on the water. We are not informed how far Peter walked toward Christ. Farrar has well explained: "And over the vessel's side into the troubled waves he sprang, and while his eye was fixed on his Lord, the wind might toss his hair, and the spray might drench his robes, but all was well; but when, with wavering faith, he glanced from Him to the furious waves, and to the gulfy blackness underneath, then he began to sink, and in an accent of despair—how unlike his former confidence!—he faintly cried, 'Lord, save me!' nor did Jesus fail. Instantly, with a smile of pity, He stretched out His hand, and grasped the hand of His drowning disciple with the gentle rebuke, 'O thou of little faith, why didst thou doubt?' And so, his love satisfied, but his over-confidence rebuked, they climbed—the Lord and His abashed Apostle—into the boat; and the wind lulled, and amid the ripple of the waves upon the moonlit shore, they were at the haven where they would be; and all—the crew as well as His disciples—were filled with deeper and deeper amazement, and some of them, addressing Him by a title which Nathanael alone had applied to Him before, exclaimed, 'Truly Thou art the Son of God.'"[126]

This expression of belief probably applied to the sailors who were on the ship. The apostles had gained a testimony that Jesus was the "Son of God" long before the miracle on the Sea of Galilee.

Regarding Simon Peter's faith faltering on the water, some individuals have characterized this as a flaw in his resolve and a weakness of his character. In answering those who find fault with the senior apostle, let them take a few steps upon the water and see how their faith compares to that of Peter's.

Though our Lord gently chided Peter on this occasion, with these words, "O thou of little faith," he knew that his senior apostle's faith was great. As the President of the Church, Peter's faith became like unto his friend and Master, even Jesus the Christ.

From what transpired on the Sea of Galilee, we observe that Peter was alert, daring, eager, and dynamic. In addition, this senior apostle was a man of action, a man of God, and most importantly, a man of faith!

Chapter Nineteen

PETER'S CONFESSION OF BELIEF
(John 1: 28, 41-42; 2: 11; Mark 9: 23; Moroni 7: 37)

Throughout the scriptures, the words *belief* and *faith* are used interchangeably. Mark, in the New Testament, has written: "All things are possible to him that believeth." Moroni, in the Book of Mormon, wrote: "It is by faith that miracles are wrought." Essentially, *belief* and *faith* mean the same thing. From their first meeting, Simon Peter "believed" that Jesus was the Messiah. By exercising "faith" in our Lord, Peter wrought the miracle of walking on the water.

In order to gain salvation, an individual must believe in Christ, which means to have faith in our Lord. Accordingly, Peter truly believed that Jesus was the Promised Messiah; therefore, he had faith in him. With this understanding, let us discover what transpired after Peter walked on the Sea of Galilee.

IN THE LAND OF GENNESARET
(Matt. 14: 34-36; Mark 6: 53-56; Acts 5: 12-15)

When the storm ended, the ship landed in the district known as the land of Gennesaret. Word rapidly spread that Jesus and his apostles were in that area, and many people gathered around our Lord, "and began to carry about in beds those that were sick, where they heard he was."

Peter observed that throughout the towns where Jesus

walked, the sick and afflicted were laid in the streets, desiring that our Lord walk by them. So great was the people's faith that those who were afflicted "besought him that they might only touch the hem of his garment," that they might be cured. Accordingly, numerous people were healed, for "as many as touched were made perfectly whole."

While serving as the President of the Church, Peter—following once again the example of our Lord—performed a manifestation of healings similar to those that were performed in the land of Gennesaret: "And by the hands of the apostles were many signs and wonders wrought among the people; . . . Insomuch that they brought forth the sick into the streets, and laid them on beds and couches, that at the least the shadow of Peter passing by might overshadow some of them."

MANY DISCIPLES TURNED AWAY
(John 6: 22-66)

We now turn our attention to the day after the five thousand were fed. The multitude was surprised to discover that Jesus was no longer in that area. Word soon spread that he was in Capernaum, in company with Peter and his fellow apostles. Approaching our Lord in the synagogue, as Elder Talmage has written, "some of the most intrusive of the crowd asked, brusquely and almost rudely, 'Rabbi, when camest thou hither?'"

"In tone of impressive rebuke Jesus said unto them: 'Verily, verily, I say unto you, Ye seek me, not because ye saw the miracles, but because ye did eat of the loaves, and were filled.' Their concern was for the bread and fishes. One who could supply them with victuals [food] as He had done must not be lost sight of.

"The Master's rebuke was followed by admonition and

instruction: 'Labour not for the meat which perisheth, but for that meat which endureth unto everlasting life, which the Son of man shall give unto you: for him hath God the Father sealed.'"[127]

Jesus went on to explain about the sermon of the bread of life and concluded with these declarative words, "I am the bread of Life." Continuing, he stated, "Verily, verily, I say unto you, Except ye eat the flesh of the Son of man, and drink his blood, ye have no life in you. Whoso eateth my flesh, and drinketh my blood, hath eternal life; and I will raise him up at the last day."

"There was little excuse for the Jews," says Elder Talmage, "pretending to understand that our Lord meant an actual eating and drinking of His material flesh and blood . . . Their failure to comprehend the symbolism of Christ's doctrine was an act of will, not the natural consequence of innocence ignorance. To eat the flesh and drink the blood of Christ was and is to believe in and accept Him as the literal Son of God and Savior of the world, and to obey His commandments."[128]

Present in the synagogue were some of the rulers—Pharisees, scribes, and rabbis. Not only were the official class in attendance, "but those," states Elder Talmage, "who had professed some measure of belief in Him were affected. 'Many therefore of his disciples, when they had heard this, said, This is an hard saying; who can hear it?' Jesus . . . asked: 'Doth this offend you?' and added: 'What and if ye shall see the Son of Man ascend up where he was before?' His ascension, which was to follow His death and resurrection, is here definitely implied."[129]

After expounding those strong doctrines many "deserted Him, and from that time sought Him no more. The occasion was crucial; the effect was that of sifting and separation."[130]

"THOU HAST THE WORDS OF ETERNAL LIFE"
(John 6: 66-71)

It appears that even the Twelve were unable to comprehend the deeper meaning of these latest teachings; they were puzzled, though none actually deserted.[131] Testing their allegiance, our Lord asked this searching question of the apostles, "Will ye also go away?"

Peter, the dynamic man of action and faith, speaking for himself and his fellow apostles, answered with this sincere confession of belief: "Lord, to whom shall we go? thou hast the words of eternal life. And we believe and are sure that thou art that Christ, the Son of the Living God"

Two years had passed since Andrew found his brother, Simon Peter, and declared with excitement and conviction, "We have found the Messias." Exhibiting a trait that would exemplify his life in the ministry of our Lord, Peter believed the words of Andrew. After meeting the Messiah, Jesus bestowed a new name upon him; thereafter, he became known as Peter, the Rock and the Seer. From that time forward, he believed that Jesus was the Promised Messiah.

Now, as the senior apostle, Peter confessed a belief that was acquired from thousands of hours of association with his beloved Lord and Master. It was not a new belief; it was a fervent reaffirmation of that which had long been in his heart and had been spoken by him on many other occasions. Peter's testimony demonstrated that he was true to our Lord, notwithstanding that many disciples had separated from the fold and "walked no more with him."

With conviction, Peter honestly declared, "We believe and are sure that thou art that Christ, the Son of the Living God." Accordingly, this believing apostle had faith in the divinity of our Lord.

112

Preparing the Twelve for his pending death and crucifixion, Jesus did not respond to Peter's great confession. Instead, he revealed this information about one of their own: "Have not I chosen you twelve, and one of you is a devil?" The apostle John explains who our Lord was speaking of: "He spake of Judas Iscariot the son of Simon: for he it was that should betray him, being one of the twelve."

CHAPTER TWENTY

PETER AND THE LAW OF CLEANLINESS
(Matt. 15: 1-20; Mark 7: 1-23; Luke 6: 39; John 6: 66)

Not only was it a time of "sifting and separation" of many weak followers, it was also a period of darkening opposition from the ruling class. As has been written previously, Peter's sincere confession of belief demonstrated that he was true to our Lord, notwithstanding that many disciples had separated from the fold and "walked no more with him."

Regarding that time, it was the season of the third Passover in the life of our Lord—April of A.D. 32. At the next yearly Passover, Jesus would be betrayed by Judas Iscariot, and suffer death by crucifixion.

As Edersheim has well explained: "And, the greater the popular expectancy and disappointment had been, the greater the reaction and the enmity that followed. The hour of decision was past, and the hand on the dial pointed to the hour of His death."[132]

"True," as Elder Talmage has written, "He [Jesus] had been repeatedly criticized and openly assailed by complaining Jews on many earlier occasions . . . . The last year of His earthly ministry was inaugurated by a sifting of the people who professed to believe His word, and this process of test, trial, and separation, was to continue to the end."[133]

Regarding this third Passover, the increasing opposition toward our Lord and his fellow apostles is made more evident by the words of Farrar:

"If Jesus attended this Passover, He must have done so in strict privacy and seclusion, and no single incident of His visit has been recorded. It is more probable that the peril and opposition which He had undergone in Jerusalem were sufficient to determine His absence . . . It is not, however, impossible that, if He did not go in person, some at least of His disciples fulfilled this national obligation; and it may have been an observation of their behavior, combined with the deep hatred inspired by His bidding the healed man take up his bed on the Sabbath day, and by the ground which He had taken in defending Himself against that charge, which induced the Scribes and Pharisees of Jerusalem to send some of their number to follow His steps, and to keep an espionage upon His actions, even by the shores of His own beloved lake. Certain it is that henceforth, at every turn and every period of His career—in the corn-fields, in synagogues, in feasts, during journeys, at Capernaum at Magdala, in Peraea, at Bethany—we find Him dogged, watched, impeded, reproached, questioned, tempted, insulted, conspired against by these representatives of the leading authorities of His nation, of whom we are repeatedly told that they were not natives of the place, but 'certain which came from Jerusalem.'"[134]

Peter observed that certain scribes and Pharisees, which lived in Jerusalem, approached Jesus and asked, "Why do thy disciples transgress the tradition of the elders? for they wash not their hands when they eat bread."

"Mark tells us," as Elder Talmage explains, "that the disciples were charged with having eaten with 'defiled,' or, as the marginal reading gives it, with 'common' hands; and he interpolates the following concise and lucid note concerning the custom which the disciples were said to have ignored: 'For the Pharisees, and all the Jews, except they wash their hands oft, eat not, holding the tradition of the elders. And when they come from the market, except they wash, they eat not. And many other things there be, which they have received to hold, as the washing of cups, and pots, brasen vessels, and of tables.' It should be borne in mind that the offense charged against the disciples was that of ceremonial uncleanness, not physical uncleanliness or disregard of sanitary propriety; they were said to have eaten with common or defiled hands, not specifically with dirty fingers . . . .

"Jesus gave no direct reply; but asked as a rejoinder: 'Why do ye also transgress the commandment of God by your tradition?'"[135]

Mark also says, "And when he [Jesus] had called all the people unto him, he said unto them, Hearken unto me every one of you, and understand: There is nothing from without a man, that entering into him can defile him: but the things which come out of him, those are they that defile the man. If any man have ears to hear, let him hear."

"The apostles," in the words of Elder Talmage, "were not sure that they understood the Master's lesson; though couched in plain, non-figurative language, it was to some of them very like a parable."[136]

After expounding other meaningful teachings to the multitude, Jesus and his disciples "entered into the house [away] from the people." Regarding the question asked by certain scribes and Pharisees, "Why do thy disciples transgress the tradition of the elders? for they wash not their hands when they eat bread," Matthew reveals: "Then answered Peter and said unto him, Declare unto us this parable."

As a teaching lesson, Jesus answered Peter, as well as his fellow apostles: "Are ye also yet without understanding? Do not ye yet understand, that whatsoever entereth in at the mouth goeth into the belly, and is cast out into the draught? But those things which proceed out of the mouth come forth from the heart; and they defile the man. For out of the heart proceed evil thoughts, murders, adulteries, fornications, thefts, false witness, blasphemies: These are the things which defile a man: but to eat with unwashen hands defileth not a man."

Mark says, "And he saith unto them, Are ye so without understanding also? Do ye not perceive, that whatsoever thing from without entereth into the man, it cannot defile him; Because it entereth not into his heart, but into the belly, and goeth out into the draught, purging all meats? And he said, That which cometh out of the man, that defileth the man. For from within, out of the heart of men, proceed evil thoughts, adulteries, fornications, murders, thefts, covetousness, wickedness, deceit, lasciviousness, an evil eye, blasphemy, pride, foolishness: All these evil things come from within, and defile the man."

"PURGING ALL MEATS"
(Mark 7: 1-23; Acts 10)

Regarding "purging all meats," Peter, as the President of the Church, received a vision to take the gospel to the Gentiles by the following representation:

"Cornelius," who was classified as a Gentile, "saw in a vision" an "angel of God coming in to him, and saying unto him . . . send men to Joppa, and call for one Simon, whose surname is Peter." Cornelius "called two of his household servants, and a devout soldier of them that waited on him continually; and when he had declared all these things unto them, he sent them to Joppa.

"On the morrow, as they went on their journey, and drew nigh unto the city, Peter went up upon the housetop to pray about the sixth hour: And he became very hungry, and would have eaten: but while they made ready, he fell into a trance, And saw heaven opened, and a certain vessel descending unto him, as it had been a great sheet knit [or bound] at the four corners, and let down to the earth: Wherein were all manner of fourfooted beasts of the earth, and wild beasts, and creeping things, and fowls of the air. And there came a voice to him, Rise, Peter; kill, and eat.

"But Peter said, Not so, Lord; for I have never eaten any thing that is common or unclean.

"And the voice spake unto him again the second time, What God hath cleansed, that call not thou common. This was done thrice: and the vessel was received up again into heaven."

When Peter met Cornelius and some of his relatives and friends, Peter "said unto them, Ye know how that it is an unlawful thing for a man that is a Jew to keep company, or come unto one of another nation; but God hath shewed me that I should not call any man common or unclean."

"Then Peter opened his mouth, and said, Of a truth I perceive that God is no respecter of persons: But in every nation he that feareth him, and worketh righteousness, is accepted with him."

Therefore, by our Lord explaining to Peter and his fellow apostles about "purging all meats" (or making all meats clean), Jesus did away with the Mosaic restrictions of ceremonial uncleanness. Then, as President of the Church, Peter—because of his vision of the beasts (or meat), who were pronounced clean—introduced the gospel of Jesus Christ to the Gentiles.

Chapter Twenty-One

PETER TESTIFIED:
"THOU ART THE CHRIST"
(Matt. 16: 13-20; Mark 8: 27-30; Luke 9: 18-21; JST Luke 9: 20; Moses 6: 57)

Despite the rising opposition from Pharisees, Sadducees, Herodians, and the scribes, Jesus and his apostles continued their Galilean ministry. They traveled to many towns and cities, wherein many people were taught the gospel and healed of their various illnesses and afflictions.

In company with Peter and the Twelve, Jesus traveled northward to an area known as the "coasts of Caesarea Philippi." This was not a coastal area by a body of water, but as Elder Talmage explains, it was "an inland city situated near the eastern and principal source of the Jordan, and near the foot of Mount Hermon."[137] As Luke has written, Jesus and his disciples went "into the towns of Caesarea Philippi." Luke also explains that when Jesus was "alone praying, his disciples were with him." This was a private meeting, away from the masses of people who constantly sought attention from our Lord. It was a special meeting of sharing testimonies and receiving spiritual instruction. Jesus then "asked his disciples" this searching question, "Whom do men say that I the Son of man am?"

The name-titles "Son of God" and "Son of Man" are identical in meaning. Regarding Jesus calling himself the Son of Man, we turn to a writing of Moses, as recorded in *The Pearl of Great Price*. According to the language of Adam, we discover that the name of Elohim, who is the Father, is "Man of Holiness." And, "the name of his Only Begotten" in the flesh is the "Son of Man." In other words, Jesus is the Son of the Man of Holiness, or the shortened version, Son of Man.

In replying to Jesus' question, "Whom do men say that I am?" The apostles answered, "Some say that thou art John the Baptist: some, Elias; and others, Jeremias, [Jeremiah] or one of the old prophets is risen again."

Our Lord then asked, "But whom say ye that I am?"

"Answering for all," as Elder Talmage has explained, "but more particularly testifying as to his own conviction, Peter, with all the fervor of his soul, voiced the great confession: 'Thou art the Christ, the Son of the living God.'"[138]

In addition to associating with our Lord for countless number of hours, Peter's confession was obtained from a higher source. To explain: the Holy Ghost is a revelator. His mission is to bear witness of God the Father and his Son, Jesus Christ. In our dispensation, the Prophet Joseph Smith revealed this great truth: "To some it is given by the Holy Ghost to know that Jesus Christ is the Son of God" (D&C 46: 13). Accordingly, our Lord spoke those revealing words to his senior apostle: "Blessed art thou, Simon Bar-jona: for flesh and blood hath not revealed it unto thee, but my Father which is in heaven."

"SIMON BAR-JONA"
(John 1: 42; Moses 6: 57)

The title "Simon Bar-jona" meant that Simon was the son of Jona. This designation was used to contrast Peter's mortal birth with Jesus' birth as the literal Son of an immortal father. Our Lord was the Son of the Man of Holiness; Simon Peter was the son of a mortal man, Jona.

"FLESH AND BLOOD"

The Lord's expression "flesh and blood hath not revealed it unto thee, but my Father which is in heaven" meant that no mortal man had revealed this knowledge to Peter; it came by revelation from God the Father, by the power of the Holy Ghost.

This was not a new belief expressed by Peter; however, it was a powerful testimony borne of the Spirit. With this information, let us find out what our Lord said to his senior, presiding apostle.

Chapter Twenty-Two

"AND UPON THIS ROCK
I WILL BUILD MY CHURCH"

"THAT THOU ART PETER"
(Matt. 16: 13-20)

Looking directly at Peter, our Lord declared these truth-filled words: "And I say also unto thee, That thou art Peter, and upon this rock I will build my church; and the gates of hell shall not prevail against it."

What "rock" was Christ going to build his Church? When the Messiah met Simon, he gave him a new name, *Peter*, which meant a "stone" or a "rock." From the Joseph Smith Translation of the Bible, we understand that Peter's new name meant a "seer, or stone." In the words of Elder McConkie, this great man became known as "Peter, the Rock and the Seer." Therefore, was Peter the "rock" of which Christ spoke?

To clarify what our Lord said to Peter, the Prophet Joseph Smith has revealed this great principle of truth: "And Jesus in His teachings says, 'Upon this rock I will build my Church, and the gates of hell shall not prevail against it.' What rock? Revelation."[139]

With this information, we again quote what our Lord said to Peter, inserting words into the scriptures, to make their meaning more clear:

"And Simon Peter answered and said, Thou are the Christ, the Son of the living God.

"And Jesus answered and said unto him, Blessed art thou, Simon Bar-Jona [Simon, son of Jona]: for flesh and blood [for mortal man] hath not revealed it [this knowledge] unto thee, but my Father which is in heaven [by the power of the Holy Ghost].

"And I say also unto thee, That thou art Peter [my senior apostle, who will become the President of my Church], and upon this rock ["What rock? Revelation."] I will build my church; and the gates of hell [the powers of hell] shall not prevail against it."

Our Lord then told Peter: "And I will give unto thee the keys of the kingdom of heaven: and whatsoever thou shalt bind on earth shall be bound in heaven: and whatsoever thou shalt loose on earth shall be loosed in heaven."

"The kingdom of heaven" did not mean the celestial realm where God the Father lives, but as Elder McConkie has written, "the kingdom of God on earth; the Church of Jesus Christ organized among men; the earthly kingdom designed to prepare men for the heavenly kingdom of the Father—such is the meaning of the language of our Lord."[140]

Peter was not to establish the Church; Christ's Church was already established with "apostles; and, some, prophets; and some, evangelists; and some, pastors and teachers" (See Eph. 4: 11). In every gospel dispensation, there is only one true Church upon the earth. In our dispensation, the Lord revealed to the Prophet Joseph Smith that The Church of Jesus Christ of Latter-day Saints is "the only true and living church upon the face of the whole earth" (See D&C 1: 30). The Church in these latter-days is the same Church that our Lord established in the days when he lived in mortality. The true Church is founded upon the rock of revelation, and has every key, power, priest-hood, and authority to perform the saving ordinances of the gospel of Jesus Christ.

"Keys are the right of presidency," Elder McConkie explains, "the directing, controlling, governing power. The keys of the kingdom are the power, right, and authority to preside over the kingdom of God on earth (which is the Church) and to direct all of its affairs (*Mormon Doctrine*, pp. 377-379). These keys include the sealing power, that is, the power to bind and seal on earth, in the Lord's name and by his authorization, and to have the act ratified in heaven. Thus if Peter performed a baptism by the authority of the sealing power here promised him, that ordinance would be of full force and validity when the person for whom it was performed went into the eternal worlds, and it would then admit him to the celestial heaven. Again, if Peter used these sealing keys to perform a marriage, then those so united in eternal marriage would continue as husband and wife forever. When they attain their future heaven, they would find themselves bound together in the family unit the same as they were on earth."[141]

Elder Talmage explains, "The Lord's promise, that unto Peter He would give 'the keys of the kingdom of heaven,' embodies the principle of divine authority in the Holy Priesthood, and of the commission of presidency. Allusion to keys as symbolical of power and authority is not uncommon in Jewish literature, as was well understood in that period and is generally current today. So also the analogies of binding and loosing as indicative of official acts were then usual, as they are now, particularly in connection with judicial functions. Peter's presidency among the apostles was abundantly manifest and generally recognized after the close of our Lord's mortal life."[142]

Regarding "the keys of the kingdom" given to Peter and his fellow apostles, Elder Boyd K. Packer (See Note 1, end of chapter) related an impressive experience. By way of introduction, in a book written about his life, we read these informative words: "It may seem to some to be a very bold doctrine that we talk of—a power which records or binds on earth and binds in heaven. Nevertheless, in all the ages of the world, whenever the Lord has given a dispensation of the priesthood to any man by actual revelation, or any set of men, this power has always been given" (D&C 128: 9).

Elder Packer had never forgotten an experience he and others had with President Spencer W. Kimball, the man who then held that position and those keys. After the area conference held in Copenhagen, Denmark, in 1976, President Kimball expressed a desire to visit the Vor Frue Church, where the Thorvaldsen statues of the Christus and the Twelve Apostles are housed. Elder Packer remembered:

"'Most of the group were near the rear of the chapel, where the custodian, through an interpreter, was giving some explanation. I stood with President Kimball, Elder Rex Pinegar, and President Bentine, the stake president, before the statue of Peter. In [the Apostle's] hand, depicted in marble, is a set of heavy keys. President Kimball pointed to them and explained what they symbolized. Then, in an act I shall never forget, he turned to President Bentine and with unaccustomed sternness pointed his finger at him and said with firm, impressive words, 'I want you to tell every Lutheran in

Denmark that they do not hold the keys! I hold the keys! We hold the real keys and we use them every day.'

"This declaration and testimony from the prophet so affected me that I knew I would never forget it—the influence was powerfully spiritual and the impression was physical in its impact as well.

"We walked to the other end of the chapel where the rest of the group were standing. Pointing to the statues, President Kimball said to the kind custodian who was showing us the building, 'These are the dead apostles. Here we have the living Apostles.' Pointing to me he said, 'Elder Packer is an Apostle.' He designated the others and said, 'Elder Monson and Elder Perry are Apostles, and I am an Apostle. We are the living Apostles. You read about seventies in the New Testament, and here are living seventies, Brother Pinegar and Brother Hales.'

"The custodian, who to that time had shown no particular emotion, suddenly was in tears.

"As we left that little chapel where those impressive sculptures stand, I felt I had taken part in an experience of a lifetime.'"[143]

While living in mortality, Jesus gave his chosen Twelve Apostles those sacred, binding keys. When Peter became the President of the Church, he held all the keys of the kingdom. For as the Lord has revealed to the Prophet Joseph Smith, in our dispensation, "The keys of the kingdom, . . . belong always unto the Presidency of the High Priesthood" (See D&C 81: 2). Only one man on earth at a time, the President of the Church, can exercise these keys in their fullness (See D&C 132: 7). Then, as the President of the Church, Peter delegated those keys to the apostles, seventies, and officers in Christ's true Church.

"TELL NO MAN THAT HE WAS
JESUS THE CHRIST"
(Matt. 16: 20; Mark 8: 30)

Returning again to the narrative, wherein Peter and his fellow apostles were given the "keys of the kingdom," both Matthew and Mark tell us that our Lord charged the apostles "that they should tell no man that he was Jesus the Christ." For two and a half years, his chosen apostles had openly testified that our Lord was the Promised Messiah. Jesus, himself, had publicly declared that he was the Son of Man. Now, opposition from the ruling class was so great, their hatred so strong, that wisdom dictated, for the present time, not to publicly bear witness that he was the Christ. Our Lord still had many important things to accomplish before his appointed death.

NOTE

Elder Boyd K. Packer was set apart as Acting President of the Quorum of the Twelve Apostles on June 5, 1994, and again March 12, 1995. He was sustained as an Assistant to the Twelve on September 30, 1961; sustained to the Quorum of the Twelve on April 6, 1970, and ordained an apostle on April 9, 1970, at age 45.

Chapter Twenty-Three

PETER COUNSELS JESUS
(Matt. 16: 21-23; Mark 8: 31-33; Luke 9: 21-22; John 3: 16-17)

We have seen Peter, this mighty man of faith, in different settings. He became the senior apostle; walked on the Sea of Galilee; confessed a great belief; learned about the law of cleanliness; again confessed a divine belief; and for all of this, was promised that the keys of the kingdom would be given him.

For three years, our Lord had been instructing and training this great man to become the President of his Church. Before Peter could assume the presiding, leadership role, he must receive additional training and instruction.

Regarding the training process of Peter and his fellow apostles, we use the paraphrased words of Farrar: "We forget how necessary it was for Christ to teach and train his apostles for their future service to the world. When we compare what the apostles were when Jesus called them and how they became when he departed from them is apparent."

Though the apostles were blessed to associate with the Lord, their main mission was to elevate the world from despair and wickedness into purity and truth.[144]

As it pertains to our Lord, and the world of which Farrar spoke, we read these informative words from John: "For God so loved the world, that he gave his only begotten Son, that whosoever believeth in him should not perish, but have everlasting life. For God sent not his Son into the world to condemn the world; but that the world through him might be saved."

131

With this information, we read the words of Mark: "And he began to teach them, that the Son of man must suffer many things, and be rejected of the elders, and of the chief priests, and scribes, and be killed, and after three days rise again."

Referring to this passage of scripture, we use the paraphrased words of Edersheim: That Christ began to teach them that he was to be rejected by the rulers of Israel, slain, and to rise again the third day. And there can be as little doubt, that Christ's language (as afterwards they looked back upon it) must have clearly implied all this. Yet, Christ was usually in the habit of using symbolic language . . . . Perhaps Jesus spoke of a figurative death and resurrection, as it were, but not the terrible details literally explained. But, the realism of the words of Jesus alarmed Peter and his affection for his Lord misled his actions.[145]

With more detail, Matthew wrote that Jesus told the apostles "that he must go unto Jerusalem, and suffer many things of the elders and chief priests and scribes, and be killed, and be raised again the third day."

It needs to be emphasized that Peter was very loyal, and very protective of our Lord. In a future day, we will witness this defending behavior, in full measure. When a mob approached Jesus for the purpose of taking him into custody, Simon Peter, the dynamic man of action, drew his sword and smote off the right ear of Malchus (See John 18: 10).

Returning again to our account, wherein Jesus told his apostles that he must go to Jerusalem and suffer and die, we immediately observe the loyal and protective nature of Peter manifesting itself, for as Matthew explains: "Then Peter took him, and began to rebuke him, saying, Be it far from thee, Lord: this shall not be unto thee."

In the words of Farrar, Peter "led Him a step or two aside from the disciples, and began to advise, to instruct, to rebuke his Lord." Taking liberty with the meaning of the scriptures, our scholar wrote: "God forbid," he said; "this shall certainly not happen to thee."[146]

Though Peter's comments were sincere, he received one of the severest reprimands ever to come from his beloved friend and Lord: "But when he had turned about and looked on his disciples, he rebuked Peter, saying, Get thee behind me, Satan: for thou savourest not the things that be of God but the things that be of men."

At that time, Peter did not fully realize the reason why Jesus came to this earth. However, Jesus informed Nephi, in the *Book of Mormon*, why he was born:

"Behold I have given unto you my gospel, and this is the gospel which I have given unto you—that I came into the world to do the will of my Father, because my Father sent me. And my father sent me that I might be lifted up upon the cross; and after that I had been lifted up upon the cross, that I might draw all men unto me, that as I have been lifted up by men even so should men be lifted up by the Father, to stand before me, to be judged of their works, whether they be good or whether they be evil—And for this cause have I been lifted up; therefore, according to the power of the Father I will draw all men unto me, that they may be judged according to their works" (See 3 Ne.27: 13-15).

"GET THEE BEHIND ME SATAN"
(Matt. 16: 23; Mark 8: 33)

Regarding our Lord's strong rebuke to his senior apostle, Farrar has written these explanatory words: "Thou art a stumbling-block unto me; for thy thoughts are not the thoughts of God, but of men. This thy mere carnal and human view—this attempt to dissuade me from my 'baptism of death' is a sin against the purposes of God."[147]

Elder Talmage says: "Peter's words constituted an appeal to the human element in Christ's nature; and the sensitive feelings of Jesus were wounded by this suggestion of unfaithfulness to His trust, coming from the man whom He had so signally honored by a few moments before. Peter saw mainly as men see, understanding but imperfectly the deeper purposes of God. Though deserved, the rebuke he received was severe. The adjuration, 'Get thee behind me, Satan,' was identical with that used against the arch-tempter himself, who had sought to beguile Jesus from the path upon which He had entered, and the provocation in the two instances was in some respects similar—the temptation to evade sacrifice and suffering, though such was the world's ransom, and to follow a more comfortable way. The forceful words of Jesus show the deep emotion that Peter's ill-considered attempt to counsel if not to tempt his Lord had evoked."[148]

We are not informed of the reaction of Peter; undoubtedly, he was greatly embarrassed, as well as humbled. Suffice it to say, due to his obedient and submissive nature, we can safely believe that he realized his error, and promptly asked for and fully received forgiveness from our Lord.

"SHALL NOT TASTE OF DEATH"
(Matt. 16: 24-28; Mark 8: 34-38; 9:1; Luke 9: 23-27; John 21: 20-24; D&C 7)

In addition to the Twelve who were present when our Lord reproved Peter, other individuals were nearby. Jesus called all the people together and spoke these words: "If any man will come after me, let him deny himself, and take up his cross, and follow me." Further, "For what shall it profit a man, if he shall gain the whole world, and lose his own soul? Or what shall a man give in exchange for his soul?"

Then, a marvelous promise was spoken by Jesus: "Verily I say unto you, That there be some of them that stand here, which shall not taste of death, till they have seen the kingdom of God come with power." As far as has been revealed, only John, the apostle—one of Peter's fishing partners, as well as one of his counselors in the First Presidency—is the only person from among the Twelve and the people then assembled, who has continued to live without tasting death.

Chapter Twenty-Four

THE TRANSFIGURATION

PETER, JAMES, AND JOHN
UPON THE MOUNT OF TRANSFIGURATION
(Matt. 17: 1-9; JST Matt. 17:5; Mark 9: 2-10; JST Mark 9: 1-3, 6; Luke 9: 28-36; JST Luke 9: 28-31, 33, 36)

With the Spirit as our guide, let us learn what transpired with Peter, James, and John upon the Mount of Transfiguration. It is important to understand that the Synoptic writers—Matthew, Mark, and Luke—have only provided a small amount of information regarding those transcendent events that occurred on Mt. Hermon (See Note end of chapter).

"In the providences of the Lord," as Elder McConkie has truthfully written, "the saints know some things that the world does not know about the spiritual outpouring of divine grace that fell on the Mount of Transfiguration. But even latter-day revelation does not set forth the full account, and until men attain a higher state of spiritual understanding than they now enjoy, they will continue to see through a glass darkly and to know only in part the visionary experiences of the presiding officers of the meridian Church. That which is known, however, singles out this night as one of the most important and glorious in the lives of those who saw within the veil and who heard the voices of the heavenly participants."[149]

"AFTER SIX DAYS"

From what has been revealed, let us reconstruct, as best we can, the events that transpired upon the mountain. Both Matthew and Mark state that the Transfiguration occurred "after six days" following the time of Peter's great confession that Jesus was the Christ. Luke, however, says it was "about an eight days" interval. Regarding the differing days, Edersheim says, "Perhaps it was the Sabbath when Peter's great confession was made; and the 'six days' of St. Matthew and St. Mark become the 'about eight days' of St. Luke, when we reckon from that Sabbath to the close of another, and suppose that at even [evening] the Saviour ascended the Mount of Transfiguration with the three Apostles: Peter, James, and John."[150]

With another view, Elder Talmage wrote: "It is probable that the six-day period was meant to be exclusive of the day on which the earlier events had occurred and of that on which Jesus and the three apostles retired to the mountain; and that Luke's 'about an eight days' was made to include these two days. There is here no ground for a claim of discrepancy."[151]

"KEYS OF THE KINGDOM" PROMISED
(Matt. 16: 16-19; JST Mark 9:1; Luke 9: 28)

When Peter made his "great confession," Jesus promised to give him the keys of the kingdom. Whether it was six days or eight days, one week had elapsed between the day of promise and that glorious day when the keys were actually conferred upon the three presiding apostles.

The Joseph Smith Translation of Mark says, "Jesus taketh Peter, and James, and John, who asked him many questions concerning his sayings; and Jesus leadeth them up into a high mountain apart by themselves." Luke informs us that Jesus took these three up into a mountain to pray.

SEASON OF THE YEAR

According to the time frame we are using from Luke, it was either summer or autumn of A.D. 32. Regarding this time of year, Edersheim states: "The Sabbath-sun had set, and a delicious cool hung in the summer air, as Jesus and the three commenced their ascent . . . . We know not the exact direction which the climbers took, nor how far their journey went . . . . The top of Hermon in summer—and it can only be ascended in summer or autumn—is free from snow.

"On that mountain-top 'He prayed.' Although the text does not expressly state it, we can scarcely doubt, that He prayed with them, and still less, that he prayed for them . . . . And, with deep reverence be it said, for Himself also did Jesus pray."[152]

"THE SONS OF THUNDER AND THE MAN OF ROCK"

It was evening when our Lord and his chosen apostles climbed the path that led up to one of the heights on Mt. Hermon. To help us visualize this sacred event, we use the gifted words of Farrar:

"And the coolness and solitude would be still more delicious to the weariness of the Man of Sorrows after the burning heat of the Eastern day and the incessant publicity which, even in these remoter regions, thronged His steps. It was the evening hour when He ascended, and as He climbed the hill-slope with those three chosen witnesses—'the Sons of Thunder and the Man of Rock'—doubtless a solemn gladness dilated His whole soul; a sense not only of the heavenly calm which that solitary communion with His Heavenly Father would breathe upon the spirit, but still more than this, a sense that He would be supported for the coming hour by ministration not of earth, and illuminated with a light which needed no aid from sun or moon or stars. He went up to be prepared for death, and He took His three Apostles with Him that, haply, having seen his glory—the glory of the Begotten of the Father, full of grace and truth—their hearts might be fortified, their faith strengthened, to gaze unshaken on the shameful insults and unspeakable humiliation of the cross."[153]

Once this righteous band reached their selected destination "to pray," it is reasonable to believe that they conversed for several hours about his sayings, and in addition, that our Lord prepared those spiritual giants for the glorious experiences that would transpire that evening.

"WERE HEAVY WITH SLEEP"
(Luke 9: 32)

From their climb up the mountain, and the late hour of the night, it was natural for Peter, James, and John to be tired; accordingly, these three were heavy with sleep. While they were sleeping, Jesus went a short distance from them and prayed.

"There, then," as Farrar wrote, "He knelt and prayed, and as He prayed He was elevated far above the toil and misery of the world which had rejected Him. He was transfigured before them, and His countenance shone as the sun, and His garments became white as the dazzling snow-fields above them. He was enwrapped in such an aureole of glistering brilliance—His whole presence breathed so divine a radiance—that the light, the snow, the lightning are the only things to which the Evangelist can compare that celestial luster."[154]

As Luke has explained: "And as he prayed, the fashion of

his countenance was altered, and his raiment was white and glistering. And, behold, there talked with him two men, which were Moses and Elias: Who appeared in glory, and spake of his decease which he should accomplish at Jerusalem."

FULLY AWAKENED
(2 Peter 1: 16)

Peter, James, and John were fully awakened from their deep sleep by "the surpassing splendor of the scene, and gazed with reverent awe upon their glorified Lord."[155] For as Peter, himself, has stated, they "were eyewitnesses of his majesty."

To help us better visualize this glorious sight, we again use the skillful words of Farrar: "In the darkness of the night, shedding an intense gleam over the mountain herbage [vegetation, such as grass], shone the glorified form of their Lord. Beside Him, in the same flood of golden glory, were . . . which they knew or heard to be Moses and Elijah. And the Three spake together, in the stillness, of that coming decease at Jerusalem, about which they had just been forewarned by Christ."[156]

"SPAKE OF HIS DECEASE"
(Luke 9: 31; JST 9: 31; Matt. 16:21-23; Mark 8: 31-33; Luke 9: 21-22)

The King James Version of Luke says that Moses and Elijah, "spake of his decease which he should accomplish at Jerusalem." However, the Joseph Smith Translation reveals that Moses and Elijah "spake of his death, and also his resurrection, which he should accomplish at Jerusalem." Though Jesus had previously told Peter and his fellow apostles that he must go to Jerusalem "and be killed, and after three days rise again," here, upon the mount, they were taught in plainness—from two, translated prophets—of his impending death and resurrection. This message helped the apostles to know that

Jesus would soon accomplish the mission for which he came into the world to fulfill.

PETER, JAMES, AND JOHN WERE TRANSFIGURED

Regarding what transpired with the three presiding apostles, the Prophet Joseph Smith has revealed the following information: "The Priesthood is everlasting. The Savior, Moses, and Elias, gave the keys to Peter, James, and John on the mount, *when they were transfigured before him*"[157] (italics added). Besides our Lord, Peter, James, and John were also transfigured.

"Transfiguration" explains Elder McConkie, "is a special change in appearance and nature which is wrought upon a person or thing by the power of God. This divine transformation is from a lower to a higher state; it results in a more exalted, impressive, and glorious condition."[158] As it pertains to the transfiguration of the Three Nephites in the Book of Mormon, we are informed "that they were changed from this body of flesh into an immortal state, that they could behold the things of God" (See 3 Ne. 28: 13-17). Therefore, Peter, James, and John were also transfigured upon the mount, in order "that they could behold the things of God."

MOSES AND ELIJAH
(Alma 45: 18-19; *Doctrines of Salvation*, Vol. 2, p. 107-111; D&C 110: 11-16; *Teachings of the Prophet Joseph Smith*, pp. 172, 323, 330-335)

Both Moses and Elias—who was Elijah—were speaking with Jesus. These ancient prophets were translated beings who had been taken into heaven without tasting death. By the laying on of hands with Jesus, Moses restored the keys of the gathering of Israel and the leading of the Ten Tribes from the land of the north. Elijah restored the keys of the sealing power in order that whatever Peter, James, and John bound or loosed on earth would be bound or loosed in heaven. In our dispensation, Moses and Elijah also conferred those same keys, by the laying on of hands, to Joseph Smith and Oliver Cowdery in the Kirtland Temple. At that appearance, those ancient prophets came as resurrected beings (See D&C 133: 55).

Specifically speaking of Peter, Elder George Q. Cannon, in 1873, spoke these words: "Peter was the senior Apostle—the President of the Twelve, and he, therefore, had the right to hold the keys, and to seal a wife to her husband, and the ordinance would be bound in heaven as he bound it on the earth."[159]

JOHN THE BAPTIST
(Matt. 14: 6-12; Mark 6: 21-29; Luke 9: 7-9; JST Mark 9: 3)

John the Baptist, who was beheaded by order of Herod the king, also appeared on the Mount of Transfiguration. For as we read in the Joseph Smith Translation of Mark: "And there appeared unto them Elias with Moses, or in other words, John the Baptist and Moses; and they were talking with Jesus." Though the gospel writers do not mention it, it appears that shortly after his appearance, John the Baptist departed.

It is important to understand that the title "Elias" was used for both Elijah and John the Baptist. Regarding the appearance of these men called "Elias," the Prophet Joseph Smith revealed: "We find the Apostles endowed with greater power than John [the Baptist]: their office was more under the spirit and power of Elijah than Elias" (*Teachings of the Prophet Joseph Smith*, p. 336). Elder Talmage explains, "The authority of Elias is inferior to that of Elijah, the first being a function of the Lesser or Aaronic order of Priesthood, while the latter belongs to the Higher or Melchizedek Priesthood."[160]

It may be that other unnamed prophets also appeared upon the Mount of Transfiguration. Someday, perhaps, we will have a full account of those individuals who appeared on that holy night.

THE FUTURE TRANSFIGURATION OF THE EARTH
(D&C 63: 20-21)

It was also revealed to the Prophet Joseph Smith that Peter, James, and John saw in vision the future transfiguration of the earth; when it will be renewed and returned to its paradisiacal state, when the Millennium will commence. For as written in the Doctrine and Covenants: "When the earth shall be transfigured, even according to the pattern which was shown unto mine apostles upon the mount; of which account the fulness ye have not yet received."

"RECEIVED THEIR ENDOWMENTS"
(*Doctrines of Salvation*, Vol. 2, p. 165; 2 Peter 1: 16-17)

According to Elder Joseph Fielding Smith, Peter, James, John "received their endowments on the mount."[161] Prior to this statement, President Heber C. Kimball, First Counselor to President Brigham Young, in 1862, stated: "Jesus took Peter, James and John into a high mountain and there gave them their endowment, and placed upon them authority to lead the Church of God in all the world . . . ."[162] Supporting this belief, Peter says that while there, they "received from God the Father honour and glory."

"MORE SURE WORD OF PROPHECY"
(2 Peter 1: 19; D&C 131: 5)

Peter, James, and John were spiritual giants. To understand their spiritual greatness, Peter declared that upon the mountain, they also received "a more sure word of prophecy." As revealed to the Prophet Joseph Smith, "The more sure word of prophecy means a man's knowing that he is sealed up unto eternal life, by revelation and the spirit of prophecy, through the power of the Holy Priesthood."

"LET US MAKE THREE TABERNACLES"
(Matt. 17: 4; Mark 9: 5; Luke 9: 33; JST Luke 9: 33)

From the Joseph Smith Translation of Luke, we obtain the following information: "And after the two men departed from him, Peter said unto Jesus, Master, it is good for us to be here; let us make three tabernacles; one for thee, and one for Moses, and one for Elias; not knowing what he said." Mark says, "For he [Peter] wist not what to say; for they were sore afraid."

"Undoubtedly," Elder Talmage has written, "Peter and his fellow apostles were bewildered, 'sore afraid' indeed; and this condition may explain the suggestion respecting the three tabernacles. 'He wist not what to say;' yet, though his remark appears confused and obscure, it becomes somewhat plainer when we remember that, at the annual feast of Tabernacles, it was customary to erect a little bower, or booth of wattled boughs, for each individual worshiper, into which he might retire for devotion."[163]

"THIS IS MY BELOVED SON"
(Matt. 17: 5-6; JST Matt. 17:5; Mark 9: 7; JST Mark 9: 6; Luke 9: 34-35)

Luke says, "While he [Peter] thus spake, there came a cloud, and overshadowed them: and they feared as they entered into the cloud. And there came a voice out of the cloud, saying, This is my beloved Son: hear him."

Matthew wrote, "While he yet spake, behold, a bright cloud overshadowed them: and behold a voice out of the cloud, which said, This my beloved Son, in whom I am well pleased; hear ye him."

Concerning this cloud, Elder McConkie has written: "Not a watery cloud, but what the Jews called the *Shekinah* or *Dwelling* cloud, the cloud which manifested the presence and glory of God. This cloud had rested upon the tabernacle in the wilderness (Num. 9: 15-22), had covered Jehovah when he visited his people (Ex. 33: 9-11; Num. 11: 25), and is the one which enveloped Jesus, after his resurrection, when he ascended to his Father (Acts 1: 9)"[164] (italics in quotation).

It was Elohim, the Eternal Father, who spoke those glorious and declarative words, "This is my beloved Son, in whom I am well pleased; hear ye him." At the sound of that voice of Supreme Majesty, Peter, James, and John "were sore afraid," and fell to the ground. We can properly believe that Jesus was able to see his Father; however, we are left without knowledge if Peter, James, and John were granted that great privilege.

With kindness and respect, "Jesus came and touched them, and said, Arise, and be not afraid." From the Joseph Smith Translation of Mark, we learn that they arose, and "when they had looked round about with great astonishment, they saw no man any more, save Jesus only, with themselves. And immediately they departed."

We are not informed how long Jesus and his chosen apostles were on the mount. Evidently, they spent most of the night and part of the early morning enwrapped in the visions of eternity.

"TELL NO MAN"
(JST Mark 9: 7; Mark 9: 9; 2 Peter 1: 16-18)

The Joseph Smith Translation of Mark says, "And as they came down from the mountain, he charged them that they should tell no man what things they had seen till the Son of Man was risen from the dead." Not even their fellow apostles were to know of the glorious events that transpired that sacred night. Evidently they were not yet prepared to understand or receive the glorious truths that were revealed, in the words of Peter, upon the "holy mount."

When Peter was the President of the Church, he explained to the members what transpired that wondrous night: "For we have not followed cunningly devised fables, when we made known unto you the power and coming of our Lord Jesus Christ, but were eyewitnesses of his majesty. For he received from God the Father honour and glory, when there came such a voice to him from the excellent glory, This is my beloved Son, in whom I am well pleased. And this voice which came from heaven we heard, when we were with him in the holy mount."

"RISING FROM THE DEAD"
(Mark 9: 9-10; Luke 9: 37)

The next day, as Jesus and his chosen three walked the path leading from the mountain to the valley floor, Mark says the apostles were "questioning one with another what the rising from the dead should mean." From what was spoken by Moses and Elijah, as written in the Joseph Smith Translation of Luke, it was made clear to Peter, James, and John that Jesus should die and be resurrected. It is important to note that the doctrine of the resurrection was not a new doctrine to the apostles. Using the words of Elder McConkie, we gather the following

147

insight: "Their questions must have been the kind any believing disciples would have asked in similar circumstances: When will the resurrection be? How will it be brought to pass? With what body will we arise? Where do resurrected beings dwell? Does the family unit continue among them? And so forth. Like questions can be heard to this day in the congregations of the saints."[165]

Truly the "Sons of Thunder and the Man of Rock" had been greatly endowed spiritually. In a future day, as the First Presidency of the Church, Peter, James, and John would fully exercise the keys of the kingdom that were conferred upon them on the holy mount.

NOTE

Regarding the place of the Transfiguration, the four scholars who are quoted throughout this work are in total agreement that it was Mt. Hermon. Therefore, I only quote the words of Elder Talmage:

"The mountain on which the Transfiguration occurred is neither named nor otherwise indicated by the gospel-writers in such a way as to admit of its positive identification. Mount Tabor, in Galilee, has long been held by tradition as the site, and in the sixth century three churches were erected on its plateau-like summit, possibly in commemoration of Peter's desire to make three tabernacles or booths, one each for Jesus, Moses, and Elijah. Later a monastery was built there. Nevertheless, Mt.Tabor is now rejected by investigators, and Mt. Hermon is generally regarded as the place. Hermon stands near the northerly limits of

Palestine, just beyond Caesarea Philippi, where Jesus is known to have been a week before the Transfiguration. Mark (9: 30) distinctly tells us that after His descent from the mount, Jesus and his apostles departed and went through Galilee. Weight of evidence is in favor of Hermon as the Mount of Transfiguration, though nothing that may be called decisive is known in the matter" (*Jesus the Christ*, 1962 ed., Note 3, p. 376).

Chapter Twenty-Five

PETER AND THE TEMPLE TAX

"FROM SUNSHINE INTO SHADOW"
(Matt. 17: 14-21; Mark 9: 14-29; Luke 9: 37-43)

It was the dawn of a new day when Peter, James, and John, in company with our Lord, descended from the mountain. The previous evening, this righteous party had enjoyed glorious experiences while on the holy mount. However, as Lehi has explained in the *Book of Mormon*, "For it must needs be, that there is an opposition in all things" (See 2 Ne. 2: 11). Even during that transcendent night, Moses and Elijah had plainly spoken of Jesus' death and resurrection, which should be accomplished at Jerusalem. It is important to realize that when those glorious, spiritual experiences ended on the Mount of Transfiguration, Peter, James, John, along with our beloved Lord, had to once again encounter the trials and tribulations that all people experience upon this earth.

Regarding this contrast, Edersheim has explained, "On Hermon the Lord and His disciples had reached the highest point in this history. Henceforth it is a descent into the Valley of Humiliation and Death!"[166]

Using similar expressions of Edersheim, Elder Talmage wrote this explanation of Jesus: "Our Lord's descent from the holy heights of the Mount of Transfiguration was more than a physical return from greater to lesser altitudes; *it was a passing from sunshine into shadow*, from the effulgent glory of heaven to the mists of worldly passions and human unbelief; it was the beginning of His rapid descent into the valley of humiliation"[167] (italics added).

At the base of the mountain, Peter, James, and John witnessed that their fellow apostles were with a multitude of people, including scribes and rabbis. "There was," as Elder Talmage says, "evidence of disputation and disturbance amongst the crowd; and plainly the apostles were on the defensive. At the unexpected approach of Jesus many of the people ran to meet Him with respectful salutations. Of the contentious scribes He asked, 'What question ye with them?' thus assuming the burden of the dispute . . . . The scribes remained silent; their courage had vanished when the Master appeared."[168]

"Then out of the crowd," as Farrar has written, "struggled a man, who, kneeling before Jesus, cried out, in a loud voice, that he was the father of an only son whose demoniac possession was shown by epilepsy, in its most raging symptoms, accompanied by dumbness, atrophy, and a suicidal mania. He had brought the miserable sufferer to the disciples to cast out the evil spirit, but their failure had occasioned the taunts of the Scribes."[169]

Jesus exclaimed, "O faithless and perverse generation, how long shall I be with you, and suffer you? Bring thy son hither."

Our Lord then asked the man how long his son had been afflicted. The father replied that it had been since he was a child. Giving further explanation, as Mark has written, he continued, "And ofttimes it hath cast him into the fire, and into the waters, to destroy him."

We may properly suppose that the next words that were spoken by this man brought a flood of memories back to Peter. As we remember, while Jesus was standing on the Sea of Galilee, in the midst of a tumultuous storm, Peter had spoken these words: "Lord, if it be thou, bid me come unto thee on the water" (See Matt. 14: 28). As was previously written in that chapter: There is not much faith expressed in the phrase "if it be thou."

"BUT IF THOU CANST"

Returning again to narrative of the demoniac boy, the father said to Jesus, "but if thou canst do any thing, have compassion on us and help us." Though spoken innocently, the man had thoughtlessly used the word "if."

Our Lord felt no need to explain his ability to heal the afflicted boy. Instead, to help increase the faith of the boy's father, Jesus replied, "If thou canst believe, all things are possible to him that believeth."

With tears in his eyes, the father answered with these twofold feelings of his heart, "Lord, I believe; help thou mine unbelief."

"DEAF AND DUMB SPIRIT"
(Mark 9: 17, 25; JST Mark 9: 22)

Jesus "rebuked the foul spirit, saying unto him, Thou dumb and deaf spirit, I charge thee, come out of him, and enter no more into him."

It is important to understand that all spirits are well and whole and have no disabilities or deformities. To support this statement, Alma, in the Book of Mormon, wrote these declarative words: "The spirit and the body shall be reunited again in its perfect form; both limb and joint shall be restored to its proper frame . . . Now, this restoration shall come to all, both old and young . . . both male and female . . . even there shall not so much as a hair of their heads be lost; but every thing shall be restored to its perfect frame . . ." (See Alma 11: 43-44). We further learn from the Joseph Smith Translation of Mark that the words *"dumb and deaf spirit"* are eliminated. Therefore, this scripture reads that Jesus "rebuked the foul spirit, saying unto him, I charge thee to come out of him, and enter no more into him."

After the Lord "rebuked the foul spirit," and by laws not revealed, "the spirit cried, and rent him sore, and come out of him: and he was as one dead; insomuch that many said, He is dead. But Jesus took him by the hand, and lifted him up; and he arose."

"PRAYER AND FASTING"

"The people were amazed," as Elder Talmage has written, "at the power of God manifested in the miracle; and the apostles who had tried and failed to subdue the evil spirit were disturbed. While on their mission, though away from their Master's helpful presence, they had successfully rebuked and cast out evil spirits as they had received special power and commission to do; but now, during his absence of a day they had found themselves unable. When they had retired to the house, they asked of Jesus, 'Why could not we cast him out?' The reply was: 'Because of your unbelief;' and in further explanation the Lord said, 'Howebeit this kind goeth not out but by prayer and fasting.'"[170]

Peter and his fellow apostles were taught a great lesson that day. Though these chosen men had been given the priesthood, they were instructed that certain afflictions required the combined efforts of fasting and prayer.

THE APOSTLES TOLD OF JESUS'
DEATH AND RESURRECTION
(Matt. 17: 22-23; Mark 9: 30-32; JST Mark 9: 27-28; Luke 9: 43-45)

Following this miracle, the Twelve traveled with Jesus and passed through Galilee. They were traveling toward Capernaum, the home of Peter, Andrew, Philip, and Matthew. Regarding this journey, the Joseph Smith Translation of Mark says, "And they departed thence, and passed through Galilee privately; for he would not that any man should know it."

During this journey, our Lord told his apostles, "Let these sayings sink down into your ears." Speaking as though he was witnessing those pending events, he declared, "The Son of Man is delivered into the hands of men, and they shall kill him; and after that he is killed, he shall rise the third day."

"We read with some surprise," states Elder Talmage, "that the apostles still failed to understand. Luke's comment is 'But they understood not this saying, and it was hid from them, that they perceived it not: and they feared to ask him of that saying.'"[171]

It is reasonable to believe that Peter, James, and John understood "this saying," though the other nine apostles did not. In support of this belief, we remember that upon the Mount of Transfiguration, Moses and Elijah had plainly spoken of Jesus' "death, and also his resurrection, which he should accomplish at Jerusalem" (See JST Luke 9: 31).

THE TEMPLE TAX MIRACULOUSLY PROVIDED
(Matt. 17: 24-27; JST Matt. 17: 24)

Our Lord and his chosen apostles were again in Capernaum. As was his custom, Jesus stayed in the home of

Peter. During a brief stay in this beautiful city, Peter was taught another great lesson regarding the divinity of our Lord from the temple tax that was miraculously provided.

Concerning this tax, we turn to Farrar for understanding:

"From time immemorial there was a precedent for collecting, at least occasionally, on the recurrence of every census, a tax of 'half a shekel' . . . of every Jew who had reached the age of twenty years, as a 'ransom for his soul,' unto the Lord. This money was devoted to the service of the Temple, and was expended on the purchase of the sacrifices, scapegoats, red heifers, incense, shewbread, and other expenses of the Temple service . . . This tax was paid by every Jew in every part of the world, whether rich or poor; and, as on the first occasion of its payment, to show that the souls of all . . . are equal before God, 'the rich paid no more, and the poor no less.' It produced vast sums of money, which were conveyed to Jerusalem by honorable messengers."[172]

With another point of view, Elder Talmage has explained:

"The annual capitation tax here referred to amounted to half a shekel or a didrachm, corresponding to about thirty-three cents in our money [as of the year 1915]; and this had been required of every male adult in Israel since the days of the exodus . . . . This tribute, as prescribed through Moses, was originally known as 'atonement money,' and its payment was in the nature of a sacrifice to accompany supplication for ransom from the effects of individual sin. At the time of Christ the annual contribution was usually collected between early March and the Passover. If Jesus was subject to this tax, He was at this time several weeks in arrears."[173]

Writing of this annual tax, Farrar asks this intriguing question, "Why had our Lord not been asked for this contribution in previous years? And why was it now demanded in autumn, at the approach of the Feast of Tabernacles, instead of in the month Adar, some six months earlier?"[174]

Suffice it to say, whether this tax was several weeks in arrears, or six months late, the collectors of the temple tax approached Peter and asked respectfully, "Doth not your master pay tribute?" It is worth noting that even the collectors were aware that Peter was the senior member of the Twelve, and that is why they asked of him the question regarding the tribute.

As Farrar has explained, "The fact that the collectors inquired of St. Peter instead of asking Jesus Himself, is another of the very numerous indications of the awe which He inspired even into the heart of His bitterest enemies . . . . But Peter, with his usual impetuous readiness, without waiting, as he should have done, to consult His Master, replied, 'Yes.'" Considering Peter's response, Farrar has further written, "If he had thought a moment longer—if he had known a little more—if he had even recalled his own great confession so recently given—his answer might not have come so glibly [convincingly]."[175]

In defense of Peter—and as has previously been written in this work—he was very loyal and protective of our Lord. This senior apostle always spoke highly of his beloved Lord and friend. By his affirmative reply, Peter wanted to explain to the collectors, in a positive manner, that his Master would comply with the required tax.

Regarding Jesus paying the temple tax, we again use the

words of Farrar: "This money was, at any rate, in its original significance, a redemption-money for the soul of each man; and how could the Redeemer, who redeemed all souls by the ransom of His life, pay this money-ransom for his own? And it was a tax for the Temple services. How, then, could it be due from Him . . . ?"[176]

The conversation between the collectors and the senior apostle must have been close to Peter's residence. Upon entering his home, Peter was met by Jesus who immediately asked him this searching question, "What thinkest thou, Simon? of whom do the kings of the earth take custom or tribute? of their own children, or of strangers?"

With awareness of his recent comments to the collectors, Peter answered respectfully, "Of strangers."

"Peter must have seen the inconsistency of expecting Jesus, the acknowledge Messiah," states Elder Talmage, "to pay atonement money, or a tax for temple maintenance, inasmuch as the temple was the House of God, and Jesus was the Son of God, and particularly since even earthly princes were exempt from capitation dues. Peter's embarrassment over his inconsiderate boldness, in pledging payment for his Master without first consulting Him, was relieved, however, by Jesus, who said: 'Notwithstanding, lest we should offend them, go thou to the sea, and cast an hook, and take up the fish that first cometh up; and when thou has opened his mouth, thou shalt find a piece of money: that take, and give unto them for me and thee.'"[177]

Once again Peter was embarrassed over his actions. Though he always spoke boldly regarding his convictions, the senior apostle, at this particular moment, humbly and respectfully complied with our Lord's request.

It is important to understand, as Elder Talmage has explained, "The money was to be paid, not because it could be rightfully demanded of Jesus, but lest non-payment give offense and furnish to His opponents further excuse for complaint. The 'piece of money,' which Jesus said Peter would find in the mouth of the first fish that took his bait, is more correctly designated by the literal translation 'stater,' indicating a silver coin equivalent to a shekel, or two didrachms, and therefore the exact amount of the tax for two persons. 'That take, and give unto them for me and thee' said Jesus. It is notable that He did not say 'for us.' In His associations with men, even with the Twelve, who of all were nearest and dearest to Him, our Lord always maintained His separate and unique status, in every instance making the fact apparent that he was essentially different from other men. This is illustrated by His expressions 'My Father and your Father,' 'My God and your God' (See John 20: 17). He reverently acknowledged that He was the Son of God in a literal sense that did not apply to any other being."[178]

To verify the words spoken by Peter, the tribute money was paid. Truly our Lord honors the words spoken by his chosen servants. Not only was the temple tax paid for the Master, but for his senior apostle as well. This tax was provided in such a distinctive manner as to confirm to Peter, and all who learned how it was obtained, that Jesus truly was a God of Miracles. Only divine wisdom could have devised such a marvelous teaching situation. Once again Peter's testimony was impressively reaffirmed that Jesus was the Christ, by the payment of the temple tax miraculously furnished with a coin found inside a fish's mouth.

Chapter Twenty-Six

PETER'S STATEMENT ABOUT FORGIVENESS
(Matt. 18: 15-17, 21-22)

Only Matthew records the next experience of Peter. To fully understand the significance of this teaching lesson, it is important to realize that a day previous, while on their journey to Capernaum, and at a distance from Jesus, the Twelve had contended among themselves over the issue of position in the kingdom of heaven. Perhaps this contention was fueled by jealousy over Jesus only taking Peter, James, and John with him into the home of Jarius when the young girl was restored to life, and alone on Mount Hermon for what reason the others did not then know.

IN THE HOME OF PETER
(Matt 18: 1-5; Mark 9: 33-40; JST Mark 9: 31, 34-35; Luke 9: 46-50)

Back in the privacy of Peter's home, our Lord asked his chosen apostles, "What was it that ye disputed among yourselves by the way?" As the Joseph Translation of Mark says, "But they held their peace, being afraid, for by the way they had disputed among themselves who was the greatest among them."

Even Peter—who, we have observed, at times, hastily spoke before properly thinking—remained silent. The reason—he had been involved in this disputation regarding prominence in the kingdom.

"With minds still tinctured [affected] by the traditional expectation of the Messiah as both spiritual Lord and temporal King," explains Elder Talmage, "and remembering some of the Master's frequent references to His kingdom and the blessed state of those who belonged thereto, and furthermore realizing that His recent utterances indicated a near crisis or climax in His ministry, they surrendered themselves to the selfish contemplation of their prospective stations in the new kingdom, and the particular offices of trust, honor, and emolument [compensation] each most desired. Who of them was to be prime minister; who would be chancellor, who the commander of the troops? Personal ambition had already engendered jealousy in their hearts."[179]

Still seeking information regarding their individual status, Matthew wrote that the disciples asked Jesus, "Who is the greatest in the kingdom of heaven?"

Knowing their thoughts, "Jesus called a little child unto him [who we may safely suppose was either a son or a grandson of Peter] and set him in the midst of them, And said, Verily I say unto you, Except ye be converted, and become as little children, ye shall not enter into the kingdom of heaven."

Our Lord concluded his remarks by declaring, "Whosoever therefore shall humble himself as this little child, the same is greatest in the kingdom of heaven. And whoso shall receive one such little child in my name receiveth me."

As Elder Talmage has explained, "Christ would not have had His chosen representatives become *childish*; far from it, they had to be men of courage, fortitude, and force; but He would have them become *childlike*. The distinction is important"[180] (italics added).

PETER'S QUESTION

While still in Peter's home, the discussion changed to the proper method of solving the differences between brethren and the principles of Church discipline. This discussion was important, for it would be the duty and responsibility of the apostles, following the death of Jesus, to decide matters that came before the Church.

Again from Matthew, we learn what our Lord said to the Twelve: "Moreover if thy brother shall trespass against thee, go and tell him his fault between thee and him alone: if he shall hear thee, thou hast gained thy brother. But if he will not hear thee, then take with thee one or two more, that in the mouth of two or three witnesses every word may be established. And if he shall neglect to hear them, tell it unto the church: but if he neglect to hear the church, let him be unto thee as a heathen man and a publican."

Considering this teaching, Peter asked this question: "Lord, how oft shall my brother sin against me, and I forgive him? till seven times?"

Again, we rely upon Elder Talmage for understanding, "He would fain [be inclined to] have some definite limit set, and he probably considered the tentative suggestion of seven times a very liberal measure, inasmuch as the rabbis prescribed a triple forgiveness only. He may have chosen seven as the next number above three having a special Pharisaical significance."[181]

With another view, Edersheim has written these thought-provoking words: "And, if speculation be permissible, we would suggest that the brother, whose offences Peter found it so difficult to forgive, may have been none other than Judas."[182]

No matter the reason for Peter's question, according to the Joseph Smith Translation of Matthew, Jesus replied: "I say not unto thee, until seven times; but, until seventy times seven."

Therefore, Peter was powerfully instructed that there was no limit on the number of times that a member of the Church should forgive an offender, based upon the condition of true repentance. However, this policy does not apply to the Church itself. Through the Prophet Joseph Smith, the Lord has revealed that there are certain sins committed by its members that warrant them being cast out of the kingdom (See D&C 42: 24-26; 64: 12-13). Therefore, when Peter became the President of the Church, he knew the difference of personally forgiving a brother, or casting him out of the kingdom for committing a serious sin.

Chapter Twenty-Seven

PETER'S QUESTION OF REWARD

KEYS CONFERRED UPON THE REMAINING TWELVE
(Matt. 18: 18)

Continuing with his teachings in the home of Peter, Jesus spoke these words to the Twelve: "Verily I say unto you, Whatsoever ye shall bind on earth shall be bound in heaven; and whatsoever ye shall loose on earth shall be loosed in heaven."

Within a short time after Peter, James, and John, in company with Jesus, came down from the Mount of Transfiguration; and at a time prior to those words spoken in the house in Capernaum; and at an unnamed place, the remaining nine apostles received the keys of the kingdom.

Standing in a half-circle, and by the laying on hands, Jesus, Peter, James, and John conferred those same keys and powers upon those chosen men. Excepting Judas Iscariot, this quorum used them to prepare mankind for salvation and exaltation in the Celestial kingdom of God.

By the bestowal of those priesthood keys, Christ's Church was properly organized with apostles and prophets. As has been previously written in this work, keys are the right of presidency, and only one man on earth can exercise them in their fullness at one time. In a future day, Peter, as the senior apostle, would be that man.

Regarding those keys, the Lord revealed to the Prophet

Joseph Smith: "For I have conferred upon you the keys and power of the priesthood, wherein I restore all things, and make known unto you all things in due time. And verily, verily, I say unto you, that whatsoever you seal on earth shall be sealed in heaven; and whatsoever you bind on earth, in my name and by my word, saith the Lord, it shall be eternally bound in the heavens; and whosesoever sins you remit on earth shall be remitted eternally in the heavens; and whosesoever sins you retain on earth shall be retained in heaven" (See D&C 132: 45-46).

"WE HAVE FORSAKEN ALL"
(Matt. 19: 1-12, 27-30; JST Matt. 19: 28; Mark 10: 28-31; Luke 18: 28-30)

We now advance to a time when Jesus and the Twelve "departed from Galilee, and came into the coasts of Judea beyond Jordan." From this description, and those written by the scholars who are quoted in this work, we know that those special men were in the territory of Perea.

While in this location, our Lord had a conversation with a rich young ruler. Following the departure of this man, who found it so difficult to give up his great possessions, Peter, with some pride in his voice for knowing that he had forsaken wealth to follow Jesus, asked this searching question: "Behold, we have forsaken all, and followed thee; what shall we have therefore?"

"Whether he spoke for himself alone," Elder Talmage has written, "or by his use of the plural 'we' meant to include all the Twelve, is uncertain and unimportant. He was thinking of the home and family he had left, and a longing for them was pardonable; he was thinking also of boats and nets, hooks and lines, and the lucrative business for which such things stood. All these he had forsaken; what was to be his reward?"[183]

From the Joseph Smith Translation of Matthew, we learn of the great promise spoken by Jesus: "Verily I say unto you, That ye who have followed me, shall, in the resurrection, [in the regeneration, as the King James Version has it written] when the Son of Man shall come sitting on the throne of his glory, ye shall also sit upon twelve thrones, judging the twelve tribes of Israel."

Not only were the Twelve—excepting Judas Iscariot—guaranteed eternal life, those chosen men were promised that they would continue to serve in their apostolic callings in the world to come. And, with Jesus, those noble souls would become judges in Israel. We may reasonably believe that neither Peter nor his fellow apostles ever conceived of such a high and exalted reward.

The blessings of the gospel are not only for the Twelve; those blessings apply equally to all members of the Church. For as Mark has written: "And Jesus answered and said, Verily I say unto you, There is no man that hath left house, or brethren, or sisters, or father, or mother, or wife, or children, or lands, for my sake, and the gospel's, But he shall receive an hundredfold . . . ."

It is true that many individuals have sacrificed much for the gospel of Jesus Christ. Whether those sacrifices were regarded as either great or small, it meant giving up something that was important, or of great worth, for that particular moment. Whatever the situation, and in the eternal perspective of things, those sacrifices will be rewarded a hundredfold in the world to come.

PETER WAS REBUKED
(JST Mark 10: 30-31)

After expounding those wonderful truths, Jesus spoke to Peter, who, but moments earlier, had spoken words of pride for his accomplishments, and revealed this great principle: "But there are many who make themselves first, that shall be last, and the last first. This he said, rebuking Peter; and they were in the way going up to Jerusalem . . . ."

As Elder McConkie has well explained: "Though Peter had forsaken all and was assured of rewards beyond measure as a consequence, yet Jesus rebuked him for putting himself forth as an example of one who had made sacrifices for the building up of the kingdom."[184]

Lest we are tempted to find fault with Peter for making a prideful comment, we must understand that he, along with his fellow apostles, had not yet received the Holy Ghost. And, as far as the gospel writers have revealed, the senior apostle never made the same mistake twice. It is important to realize that each lesson that Peter learned helped prepare him for the great leadership role that we would soon assume.

Chapter Twenty-Eight

PETER'S COMMENT REGARDING THE FIG TREE

IN BETHANY
(Luke 10: 38-42; John 11: 1-46, 55-57; 12: 1, 9-11; Matt. 26: 6-13; Mark 14: 3-9; John 12: 2-8)

Peter was in attendance when certain events transpired during the last week of the mortal life of our beloved Lord. Because the purpose of this work is to present as accurately as possible the life of Peter, those eventful happenings will only be briefly mentioned.

According to the time frame we are using—and this is the chronology used by all of the scholars quoted in this work—it was Friday when Jesus and the Twelve left Jericho and rested in a village called Bethany. This special party was traveling toward Jerusalem to attend the annual Passover. During his visits to Bethany, Jesus always stayed in the home of his close and beloved friends, Mary and Martha, and their brother, Lazarus.

As Elder Talmage says, "Six days before the Feast of the Passover, that is to say before the day on which the Paschal lamb was to be eaten, Jesus arrived at Bethany, the home town of Martha and Mary, and of Lazarus who had recently died and been restored to life. The chronology of events during the last week of our Lord's life supports the generally accepted belief that in this year, the fourteenth day of Nisan, on which the

Passover festival began, fell on Thursday; and this being so, the day on which Jesus reached Bethany was the preceding Friday, the eve of the Jewish Sabbath. Jesus fully realized that this Sabbath was the last He would live to see in mortality."[185]

Concerning this Sabbath day, we read that while Jesus and the Twelve were in the home of this beloved family, a festive meal was prepared, and as both Matthew and Mark have written, it was "in the house of Simon the leper." According to the scholars who are quoted in this work, they have assumed that Simon was the father of the two sisters and their brother, Lazarus, and that our Lord had cured Simon's leprosy.

Martha—in Simon's home—served the honored guests; Lazarus sat at the table with Jesus; Peter and his fellow apostles, along with other faithful disciples, ate the prepared meal. It is worth noting that other curious individuals who wanted to see the raised Lazarus were also present. Sometime during this festivity, as Matthew has written, Mary anointed Jesus' head with expensive oil; John states that she anointed his feet. Following this anointing, Judas Iscariot—the one who betrayed our Lord—with "indignation" exclaimed, "Why was this waste of the ointment made? For it might have been sold for more than three hundred pence, and have been given to the poor." Jesus replied, "Let her alone; why trouble ye her? She hath wrought a good work on me. For ye have the poor with you always . . . but me ye have not always."

PETER AND JOHN SENT TO GET A COLT
(Matt. 21: 1-11; Mark 11: 1-11; Luke 19: 29-44; John 12: 12-19)

On Sunday, April 1, A.D. 33, Jesus, with Peter and his fellow apostles, left Bethany and traveled toward Jerusalem. According to Mark, "And when they came nigh to Jerusalem, unto Bethphage and Bethany, at the mount of Olives, he sendeth forth two of his disciples, And saith unto them, Go your way into the village over against you: and as soon as ye be entered into it, ye shall find a colt tied, whereon never man sat; loose him, and bring him. And if any man say unto you, Why do ye this? say ye that the Lord hath need of him; and straightway he will send him hither." Matthew wrote that they would "find an ass tied, and a colt with her: loose them, and bring them unto me."

Regarding Jesus sending "two of his disciples," Farrar provides this believable explanation: "Passing from under the palm-trees of Bethany, they approached the fig-gardens of Bethphage, the 'House of Figs,' a small suburb or hamlet of undiscovered site, which lay probably a little to the south of Bethany, and in sight of it. To this village, or some other hamlet which lay near it, Jesus dispatched two of His disciples. The . . . description of the spot given by St Mark makes us suppose that *Peter was one of them*, and if so he was probably *accompanied by John*"[186] (italics added).

In support of Farrar's supposition, we will soon read that Jesus instructed Peter and John to prepare the Passover meal (See Luke 22: 8). Therefore, it would be reasonable to believe that Peter and John were the apostles who retrieved the colt as instructed. Shortly afterwards, Jesus entered triumphantly into Jerusalem riding upon this donkey.

When evening came, as Mark says, Jesus "went out unto Bethany with the Twelve."

THE RETURN TO JERUSALEM
(Matt. 21: 18-22; Mark 11: 12-14, 20-24)

Early in the morning—on Monday, April 2—Jesus and his apostles left Bethany. They were returning to the temple in Jerusalem. Evidently, this party did not eat breakfast, for as

Mark explains, Jesus was hungry. Providing additional information, Elder Talmage has written, "Looking ahead He saw a fig tree that differed from the rest of the many fig trees of the region in that it was in full leaf though the season of fruit had not yet come . . . It would be reasonable, therefore, for one to expect to find edible figs even in early April on a tree that was already covered with leaves. When Jesus and His party reached this particular tree, which had rightly been regarded as rich in promise of fruit, they found on it nothing but leaves; it was a showy, fruitless, barren tree. It was destitute even of old figs, those of the preceding season, some of which are often found in spring on fruitful trees."[187]

For reasons of his own, Jesus cursed the tree. According to Matthew's record, our Lord said, "Let no fruit grow on thee henceforward for ever." Mark says, "No man eat fruit of thee hereafter for ever."

Matthew's gospel gives the impression that "presently the fig tree withered away." However, Mark explains that "in the morning, as they passed by, they saw the fig tree dried up from the roots." Apparently, after returning from the temple on Monday, Jesus and his apostles spent another night in Bethany. Therefore, on Tuesday, April 3, this party journeyed once again to Jerusalem. "And Peter calling to remembrance saith unto him, Master, behold, the fig tree which thou cursedst [sic] is withered away."

Though Jesus blessed the lives of many people, he had the power to curse and afflict punishment. For as was revealed to the Prophet Joseph Smith, "And again, verily I say, whomsoever you bless I will bless, and whomsoever you curse I will curse, saith the Lord; for I, the Lord, am thy God" (See D&C 132: 47).

In response to Peter's comment, Jesus revealed this doctrine: "Verily I say unto you, If ye have faith, and doubt not, ye shall not only do this which is done to the fig tree, but also if ye shall say unto this mountain, Be thou removed, and be thou cast into the sea; it shall be done. And all things, whatsoever ye shall ask in prayer, believing, ye shall receive."

Besides the experience of walking on the Sea of Galilee, Peter was impressively instructed that by faith "all things" were possible. By what happened to the fig tree, the senior apostle witnessed that faith was a principle of power that could be exercised to either bless or curse, depending upon the circumstance, as directed by an answer to prayer.

Chapter Twenty-Nine

PETER AND JOHN PREPARED
THE PASSOVER MEAL
(Matt. 26: 1-5)

TWO DAYS BEFORE JESUS' CRUCIFIXION

It was Wednesday, April 4, A.D. 33. Jesus and the Twelve had left Bethany in the morning and journeyed to the temple in Jerusalem, and in the evening, they returned to the beloved home in that little village. Considering this daily journey—and respectfully realizing that our British scholar did not have the full light of the gospel to guide him—Farrar wrote these words: "And the next day—the Wednesday in Passion week—must have baffled him. Each day Jesus had left Bethany in the morning and had gone to Jerusalem. Why did He not go on that day? Did he suspect treachery? That day in the Temple Courts the multitude listened for His voice in vain. Doubtless the people waited for Him with intense expectations; doubtless the priests and Pharisees looked out for Him with sinister hope; but He did not come. The day was spent by Him in deep seclusion, so far as we know in perfect rest and silence."[188]

With all due respect to Farrar's comments, Jesus was not "baffled." Our Lord's actions were not driven by human whims and fears. In all matters, Christ conformed his will to obey the will of his Father. In addition, every prophecy that had been spoken of him by holy men of God would be fulfilled in exact detail.

175

Therefore, we trust that in the home of his beloved friends—Mary, Martha, and their brother Lazarus—our Lord received the needed peace and companionship he earnestly sought. We are left without knowledge of what transpired that day in Bethany, excepting this one sentence written by Matthew regarding what Jesus told the Twelve: "Ye know that after two days is the feast of the Passover, and the Son of man is betrayed to be crucified."

Upon hearing that sobering pronouncement, we can well imagine the thoughts that must have passed through Peter's mind. What would he and his fellow apostles do without the guidance and instruction of their Master Teacher? As the senior apostle, what would transpire in his life after his beloved Lord was gone? What would happen to the Church following the death of its greatest Prophet? What other thoughts might have passed through Peter's mind, we are left to wonder.

JUDAS ISCARIOT
(Matt. 26: 14-16; Mark 14: 10-11; Luke 22: 3-6)

With this information, we briefly turn our attention to the man known as Judas Iscariot. Prior to the Passover, as Matthew says: "Then one of the Twelve, called Judas Iscariot, went unto the chief priests, And said unto them, What will ye give me, and I will deliver him unto you? And they covenanted with him for thirty pieces of silver. And from that time he sought opportunity to betray him [Jesus]."

Many scholars—including those who are quoted throughout this work—have written lengthy reasons for Judas's action. For the purpose of this work, I only use these short, but meaningful words written by Elder Talmage: "Before Judas sold Christ to the Jews, he had sold himself to the devil; he had become Satan's serf, and did his master's bidding."[189]

176

PETER AND JOHN SENT TO JERUSALEM
(Luke 22: 7-14)

Again from Elder Talmage, we gather the following information: "The day preceding the eating of the Passover lamb had come to be known among the Jews as the first day of the feast of the unleavened bread, since on that day all leaven [like yeast] had to be removed from their dwellings, and thereafter for a period of eight days the eating of anything containing leaven was unlawful."[190]

With this information, we read what Matthew wrote: "Now the first day of the feast of unleavened bread the disciples came to Jesus, saying unto him, Where wilt thou that we prepare for thee to eat the Passover?" Mark tells us that Jesus "sendeth forth two of his disciples" to make those arrangements.

PETER AND JOHN SENT
(Luke 22: 7-9)

From Luke, we learn that Jesus "sent Peter and John, saying, Go and prepare us the Passover, that we may eat." Accordingly, they asked the Lord, "Where wilt thou that we prepare?"

THE INSTRUCTIONS GIVEN PETER AND JOHN
(Luke 22: 10-12; Matt. 26: 18)

And Jesus answered Peter and John, as Luke explains: "Behold, when ye are entered into the city [Jerusalem], there shall a man meet you, bearing a pitcher of water; follow him into the house where he entereth in. And ye shall say unto the goodman of the house, The Master saith unto thee, Where is the guestchamber, where I shall eat the Passover with my disciples? And he shall shew you a large upper room furnished: there make ready."

Regarding this home where the Passover meal was to be eaten, Farrar has written these thought-provoking words: "Accordingly He [Jesus] sent Peter and John to Jerusalem, and appointing for them a sign both mysterious and secret, told them that on entering the gate they would meet a servant carrying a pitcher of water from one of the fountains for evening use; following him they would reach a house, to the owner of which they were to intimate the intention of the Master to eat the Passover there with His disciples; and this householder—conjecture by some to have been Joseph of Arimathaea, by others John Mark—would at once place at their disposal a furnished upper room, ready provided with the [required] table and couches." In addition, he further wrote: ". . . perhaps the very room where three days afterward the sorrow-stricken Apostles first saw their risen Saviour . . ."[191]

Edersheim says: "To us at least it seems most likely, that it was the house of Mark's father (then still alive)—a large one, as we gather from Acts 12:12."[192] Following the same reasoning, Elder McConkie also has written that "many have speculated that it was the father of John Mark."[193] No matter who that individual was, it appears evident that his name was withheld so as to keep that knowledge from Judas Iscariot. With this information, we may properly believe that Peter, John and the homeowner knew one another.

PETER AND JOHN OBEYED JESUS
(Matt. 26: 19-20; Luke 22: 13-14; 1 Peter 1: 19-20)

Obediently, Peter and John, as Matthew says, "did as Jesus had appointed them; and they made ready the Passover." Considering this preparation, Edersheim says: "We can scarcely be mistaken in supposing that Peter and John . . . had slain the [Passover] lamb. Little more remained to be done. The sacrifice was laid on staves which rested on the shoulders of Peter and John . . . . The lamb would be roasted on a pomegranate spit . . . . Everything else, also, would be made ready."[194]

We may further suppose that Peter and John carried the roasted Paschal Lamb back to the home where the Passover meal was to be eaten. Two conclusions can be drawn from Peter and John being asked to prepare this Passover: First, they were once again impressively taught that Jesus was the Son of God. Secondly, though this would be the last Passover they would prepare for our Lord, this act prepared them to accept the atoning sacrifice to be made by the Lamb of God.

Regarding Jesus being the true Paschal Lamb who was sacrificed to redeem all mankind, Peter, as the President of this Church, made this great declaration: "Forasmuch as ye know that ye were not redeemed with corruptible things, as silver and gold, from your vain conversation received by tradition from your fathers; But with the precious blood of Christ, as of a lamb without blemish and without spot."

Chapter Thirty

PETER'S FEET WASHED BY JESUS

THE LAST SUPPER
(John 13: 1-17, 20; JST John 13: 8, 10)

It was Thursday, April 5, A.D. 33, and the Passover meal was to be eaten by Peter and his fellow apostles, in company with Jesus. Concerning this day, Elder Talmage explains: "In the evening, Thursday evening as we reckon time, but the beginning of Friday according to the Jewish calendar, Jesus came with the Twelve, and together they sat down to the last meal of which the Lord would partake before His death." In an endnote, he wrote: "That He [Jesus] was crucified on Friday, the day before the Jewish Sabbath, and that He rose a resurrected Being on Sunday, the day following the Sabbath of the Jews, are facts attested by the four Gospel-writers. From the three synoptists we infer that the last supper occurred on the evening of the first day of unleavened bread, and therefore at the beginning of the Jewish Friday."[195]

Peter and John brought the roasted lamb to the large room. The homeowner—whoever he was—had prepared the unleavened cakes, bitter herbs, and dishes filled with vinegar. In addition, the festive lamps were lit, and the meal was ready to be eaten.

WHERE PETER, JOHN, AND JUDAS SAT AT THE SUPPER

Based upon scriptural allusions and inferences, Farrar has written these words regarding the seating arrangements at the meal: "They [the various artist depictions of the meal] were totally unlike those with which the genius of Leonardo da Vinci, and other great painters, has made us so familiar. The room probably had white walls, and was bare of all except the most necessary furniture and adornment. The couches or cushions, each large enough to hold three persons, were placed around three sides of one or more low tables of gaily painted wood, each scarcely higher than stools. The seat of honor was the central one of the central . . . mat. This was, of course, occupied by the Lord. Each guest reclined at full length, leaning on his left elbow, that his right hand might be free. At the right hand of Jesus reclined the beloved disciple [John], whose head therefore could, at any moment, be placed upon the breast of his friend and Lord."[196]

Edersheim says: "Sadly humiliating as it reads, and almost incredible as it seems, the Supper began with 'a contention among them, which of them should be accounted to be greatest' (See Luke 22: 24). We can have no doubt that its occasion was the order in which they should occupy places at the table. We know that this was subject of contention among the Pharisees, and that they claimed to be seated according to their rank. A similar feeling now appeared . . . in the circle of the disciples and at the Last Supper of the Lord. Even if we had no further indications of it, we should instinctively associate such a strife with the presence of Judas. St. John seems to refer to it, at least indirectly, when he opens his narrative with this notice: 'And during supper, the devil having already cast it into his

heart, that Judas Iscariot, the son of Simon, shall betray him'...
(See John 13: 2).

"From the Gospel-narratives we infer, that *St. John*
must have reclined next to Jesus, on His Right Hand,
since otherwise he could not have leaned back on His
Bosom . . . (See John 13: 23).

"In the strife of the disciples, which should be
accounted the greatest, this had been claimed, and we
believe it to have been actually occupied by *Judas*. This
explains how, when Christ whispered to John by what
sign to recognize the traitor, none of the other disciples
heard it (See John 13: 25-26). It also explains, how
Christ would first hand to Judas the sop, which formed
part of the Paschal ritual, beginning with him as the
chief guest at the table, without thereby exciting special
notice. Lastly, it accounts for the circumstance that,
when Judas, desirous of ascertaining whether his
treachery was known, dared to ask whether it was he,
and received the affirmative answer (*See* Matt 26: 25),
no one at [the] table knew what had passed. But this
could not have been the case, unless Judas had occupied the place next to Christ; in this case, necessarily
that at His [Jesus'] left . . . . As regards *Peter*, we can
quite understand how, when the Lord with such loving
words rebuked their [the apostles] self-seeking and
taught them of the greatness of Christian humility, he
should, in his impetuosity of shame, have rushed to
take the lowest place at the other end of the table.
Finally, we can now understand how Peter could
beckon to John, who sat at the opposite end of the table,
over against him, and ask him across the table, who the
traitor was (See John 13: 24). The rest of the disciples

would occupy such places as were most convenient, or suited their fellowship with one another"[197] (italics added).

PETER'S REMARKS TO JESUS
(John 13: 2-11)

John explains, "And supper being ended,"—or "during Supper," as both Edersheim[198] and Elder McConkie[199] have concluded—our Lord rose "from supper, and laid aside his garments; and took a towel, and girded himself. After that he poureth water into a [basin], and began to wash the disciples' feet, and to wipe them with the towel wherewith he was girded."

John's record gives the impression that Jesus had washed other "disciples feet" before those of Peter. However, as Elder McConkie has explained, "If we judge aright, Peter was the first one to have his feet washed, as he should have been, he being the senior apostle and the future president of the Church. John's phrase, 'Then cometh he to Simon Peter,' means, not that he came to him after the others, but either that he came to him from across the table or from the place where the basin and water for purification had stood. It would have been quite inappropriate, a self-serving assertion of excessive humility on his part, if Peter had first seen Jesus wash the feet of others and had then objected to the performances of the same act on his behalf."[200]

With this information, we read of the senior apostle's response to Jesus: "Lord, dost thou wash my feet?"

Peter's response had a two-fold meaning: First, the washing of feet was the duty of a slave. Therefore, the senior apostle objected to the Son of God, as though he were a slave, washing the feet of one who felt he was unworthy of such an act.

Secondly, it was the words spoken out of deepest reverence for the Master; yet, Peter asked our Lord a question without understanding the significance of a sacred priesthood ordinance that was being introduced. Our Lord answered: "What I do thou knowest not now; but thou shalt know hereafter."

According to the Joseph Smith Translation of John, Peter answered: "Thou needest not to wash my feet."

Jesus replied: "If I wash thee not, thou hast no part with me."

Without properly thinking, as he should have, Peter exclaimed: "Lord, not my feet only, but also my hands and my head."

Our Lord revealed: "He that has washed his hands and his head, needeth not save to wash his feet, but is clean every whit; and ye are clean, but not all."

Regarding this statement that the Twelve were "clean . . . but not all," John wrote this explanation: "For he knew who should betray him; therefore said he, Ye are not all clean. So after he had washed their feet, and had taken his garments, and was set down again, he said unto them, Know ye what I have done to you?"

To partially answer what he had done for each of the apostles, Elder Talmage wrote: "Each of them had been immersed at baptism; the washing of feet was an ordinance pertaining to the Holy Priesthood, the full import of which they had yet to learn."[201]

A SACRED PRIESTHOOD ORDINANCE
(D&C 88: 74-75, 127-141; *History of the Church*, Vol. 1, pp. 322-324; Vol. 2, p. 287, 308-309, 426, 430-431)

The washing of feet is a sacred priesthood ordinance that is usually performed in holy places. For the purpose of this work, a brief mention of this ordinance will be sufficient. On

December 27, 1832, the Prophet Joseph Smith received this revelation: "And I give unto you, who are the first laborers in this last kingdom, a commandment that you assemble yourselves together . . . and sanctify yourselves; yea, purify your hearts, and cleanse your hands and your feet before me, that I may make you clean; That I may testify unto your Father, and your God, and my God, that you are clean from the blood of this wicked generation . . . ."

With this information, it is proper to ask the following question: Did Peter and his fellow apostles fully know what our Lord had done for them? In answering, we may properly believe that the Twelve were told more than what John wrote, for the true meaning of that sacred ordinance is reserved for those who receive it.

Speaking to the Twelve who had their feet washed, our Lord gave this instruction: "Ye call me Master and Lord: and ye say well; for so I am. If I then, your Lord and Master, have washed your feet; ye also ought to wash one another's feet. For I have given you an example, that ye should do as I have done to you.

"Verily, verily, I say unto you, The servant is not greater than his lord; neither he that is sent greater than he that sent him. If ye know these things, happy are ye if ye do them."

Accordingly, Peter received the sacred ordinance of washing of feet in order that he would be "clean from the blood of [that] wicked generation." Then, when he became the President of the Church, Peter performed that special priesthood ordinance so that others would likewise be "clean."

Chapter Thirty-One

PETER'S DECLARATION OF ALLEGIANCE

PETER BECKONED TO JOHN
(Matt. 26: 21-25; Mark 14: 18-21; JST Mark 14: 30; Luke 22: 21-23; John 13: 18-19, 21-30; JST 13: 19)

At the conclusion of the ordinance of washing of feet, as Matthew has explained, our Lord made this solemn announcement to the Twelve: "Verily I say unto you, that one of you shall betray me."

Upon hearing that surprising announcement, we can imagine the thoughts that must have passed through the minds of Peter and his fellow apostles—especially Judas Iscariot. "And they [eleven of the Twelve] were exceeding sorrowful, and began every one of them to say unto him, Lord, is it I?"

Jesus replied, "He that dippeth his hand with me in the dish, the same shall betray me. The Son of Man goeth as it is written: but woe unto that man by whom the Son of Man is betrayed! It had been good for that man if he had not been born."

Ironically, Judas—with full knowledge of his betrayal—asked, "Master, is it I?" Our Lord honestly replied, "Thou hast said."

Turning our attention to John's gospel, we obtain this information: "Now there was leaning on Jesus' bosom one of his disciples, whom Jesus loved" [who was John, himself].

Desiring to know the identity of the betrayer, Peter—who was seated across the table from John—gestured to the beloved apostle to ask the Lord. For as John has written: "Simon Peter therefore beckoned to him [John], that he should ask [Jesus] who it should be of whom he spake."

Accordingly, while "lying on Jesus' breast [John] saith unto him, Lord, who is it?" Our Lord answered, "He it is, to whom I shall give a sop, when I have dipped it." And when he had dipped the sop, he gave it to Judas Iscariot, the son of Simon. Then said Jesus unto Judas, "That thou doest, do quickly."

Though the beloved apostle asked our Lord the question requested from Peter, we are left to wonder whether the senior apostle heard the answer. More than likely he did not, for as John wrote: "Now no man at the table knew for what intent he [Jesus] spake this unto him [Judas]. For some of them thought, because Judas had the [money] bag, that Jesus had said unto him, Buy those things that we have need of against the feast; or, that he should give something to the poor. He then having received the sop went immediately out: and it was night."

Regarding the sop, Edersheim has written this explanation: "But we have direct testimony, that about the time of Christ, 'the sop' which was handed round consisted of these things wrapped together: flesh of the Paschal Lamb, a piece of unleavened bread, and bitter herbs. This, we believe, was 'the sop' which Jesus, having dipped it for him in the dish, handed first to Judas . . . ."[202]

THE ORDINANCE OF THE SACRAMENT

After the departure of Judas Iscariot, Peter and the remaining apostles were introduced to another new ordinance—the partaking of the sacrament. The Joseph Smith Translation of Matthew states: "And as they were eating, Jesus took bread and brake it, and blessed it, and gave to his disciples, and said, Take, eat; this is in remembrance of my body which I give a ransom for you. And he took the cup, and gave thanks, and gave it to them, saying, Drink ye all of it. For this is in remembrance of my blood of the New Testament, which is shed for as many as shall believe on my name, for the remission of their sins. And I give unto you a commandment, that ye shall observe to do the things which ye have seen me do, and bear record of me even unto the end."

The Joseph Smith Translation of Mark says: "And as oft as ye do this ordinance, ye will remember me in this hour that I was with you, and drank with you of this cup, even the last time in my ministry."

It is important to realize that Matthew and Mark only wrote a partial account of the sacramental ordinance that was introduced by our Lord. Fortunately, from the words written in the *Book of Mormon* and the *Doctrine and Covenants*, we have a better understanding of this sacred ordinance that was introduced to eleven of the New Testament apostles.

Based upon what is done in the Church today, we may suppose that after our Lord was crucified, Peter and his fellow apostles introduced the sacramental ordinance to the members of the Church in their day; afterwards, the total membership of the Church partook of the sacrament weekly.

THE LORD'S DECLARATION
(Matt. 26: 29; Mark 14: 25)

Concluding the partaking of the emblems of the sacrament in the upper room, as Matthew has written, our Lord spoke these revealing words: "But I say unto you, I will not drink henceforth of this fruit of the vine, until that day when I drink it new with you in my Father's kingdom." Mark's record says: "Verily I say unto you, I will drink no more of the fruit of the vine, until that day that I drink it new in the kingdom of God."

THE PROMISE GIVEN TO THE PROPHET JOSEPH SMITH

The significance of this promise given to the New Testament apostles was revealed to the Prophet Joseph Smith, wherein the Lord provided this information about using water instead of wine in the sacramental services of the Church: "For, behold, I say unto you, that it mattereth not what ye shall eat or what ye shall drink when ye partake of the sacrament, if it so be that ye do it with an eye single to my glory—remembering unto the Father my body which was laid down for you, and my blood which was shed for the remission of your sins" (See D&C 27: 2).

Then, using similar words spoken to Peter and his fellow apostles at the last supper, our Lord promised the Prophet Joseph Smith: "Behold, this is wisdom in me; wherefore, marvel not, for the hour cometh that I will drink of the fruit of the vine with you on the earth" (See D&C 27: 5).

PETER, JAMES, AND JOHN TO PARTAKE
OF THE SACRAMENT

Besides the Prophet Joseph Smith, the Lord then named others who would be present to partake of the sacramental emblems in that great assembly at Adam-ondi-Ahman: Moroni, Elias, John the Baptist, Elijah, Joseph, Jacob, Isaac, Abraham, and Michael, who is Adam.

"And also with *Peter*, and *James*, and *John*, whom I have sent unto you, by whom I have ordained you and confirmed you to be apostles . . ." (See D&C 27: 6-12) (italics added).

THE PROMISE GIVEN TO THE APOSTLES
AND RIGHTEOUS SAINTS

The New Testament promise was that besides Peter, James, and John, the eleven apostles who first partook of the sacrament in the upper room would be in attendance. From the revelation given to the Prophet Joseph Smith, the Lord further revealed: "And also with all those whom my Father hath given me out of the world" (See D&C 27: 14). Therefore, all of the righteous saints of all ages will assemble to partake of the sacramental emblems with the Lord in that great congregational gathering.

AFTER JUDAS' DEPARTURE

While in the upper room, as Elder Talmage has explained, "The departure of Judas Iscariot appears to have dissipated to some degree the cloud of utter sadness by which the little company had been depressed; and our Lord Himself was visibly relieved. As soon as the door had closed upon the retreating deserter, Jesus exclaimed, as though His victory over death had been already accomplished: 'Now is the Son of Man glorified, and God is glorified in him.' Addressing the Eleven in terms of parental affection, He said: 'Little children, yet a little while I am with you. Ye shall seek me: and as I said unto the Jews, Whither I go, ye cannot come; so now I say to you. A new commandment I give unto you, That ye love one another; as I have love you, that ye also love one another. By this shall all men know that ye are my disciples, if ye have love one to another.'"[203]

THE CONVERSATION BETWEEN PETER AND JESUS

The reader is informed that John and Luke record the conversation between Peter and our Lord as occurring at the Feast of the Passover. However, Matthew and Mark have written that it transpired at the Mount of Olives, after this righteous party had left the paschal celebration. By combining

191

the gospel records, we gain a better understanding of what was spoken that evening. The discussion began with the tests that lay ahead for Peter and his fellow apostles, and of their stated allegiance to Jesus. It appears evident that during this conversation the Lord also instructed the apostles about the two comforters, the law of love, and by his offering of the great Intercessory Prayer.

FROM JOHN'S GOSPEL
(John 13: 31-38; 14: 1-6; JST John 14: 3)

With this understanding, we turn or attention to the conversation that began in the upper room at the Passover Feast. Concerning our Lord's statement, "Whither I go, ye cannot come," Peter asked sincerely: "Lord, whither goest thou?"

"Jesus answered him, Whither I go, thou canst not follow me now; but thou shalt follow me afterwards." It is noteworthy this promise informed the senior apostle that in a future day he, too, would suffer death by martyrdom (See John 21: 18-19).

Peter earnestly replied: "Lord, why cannot I follow thee now? I will lay down my life for thy sake."

"Peter seems to have realized," as Elder Talmage says, "that his Master was going to His death; yet, undeterred, he asserted his readiness to follow even that dark way rather than be separated from his Lord. We cannot doubt the earnestness of Peter's purposes nor the sincerity of his desire at that moment."[204]

PETER WAS TOLD HE WOULD DENY KNOWING JESUS
(John 13: 38)

With kindness, Jesus asked Peter this searching question: "Wilt thou lay down thy life for my sake?" Without waiting for a reply, our Lord informed the senior apostle: "Verily, verily, I say unto thee, The cock shall not crow, till thou has denied me thrice."

FROM LUKE'S GOSPEL
(Luke 22: 31-38; JST Luke 22: 31-36)

From the Joseph Smith Translation of Luke, we find out what our Lord told Peter: "Simon, Simon, behold Satan hath desired you, that he may sift the children of the kingdom as wheat." Truly Satan wanted the soul of Simon Peter. Without the guidance of the presiding apostle, how much easier it would be for the prince of darkness to destroy the faith of the members of Christ's Church. Accordingly, our Lord told this noble soul: "But I have prayed for you, that your faith fail not; and when you are converted, strengthen your brethren."

Peter had a strong testimony. On previous occasions, and by the power of the Spirit, the senior apostle had testified that Jesus was the Christ, the Son of the Living God; he had preached the gospel and baptized other believing souls; he had performed mighty miracles—one of them was walking on the water—; he had willingly forsaken his profession, his wealth, and left his beloved family home, to follow the Lord. This great man had been true and valiant to our Lord. However, Simon Peter was not yet fully converted; he had not yet become a new creature by the power of the Holy Ghost. This conversion would not occur until the day of Pentecost, when he and his fellow apostles received the gift of the Holy Ghost (See Acts 2: 1-17).

Therefore, we read that Peter, "being aggrieved," boldly declared: "Lord, I am ready to go with you, both into prison, and unto death."

Again, our Lord told Peter, "The cock shall not crow this

day, before that you will thrice deny that you know me."

Changing the subject, our Lord—who was reassuring his apostles that their physical needs would be provided for after he was gone—asked this question: "When I sent you without purse and scrip [a small bag or wallet], or shoes, lacked ye any thing?" Collectively, they answered, "Nothing." Then he stated: "I say unto you again, He who hath a purse, let him take it, and likewise his scrip; and he who hath no sword, let him sell his garment and buy one."

With these statements, our Lord revoked the commandment given previously to the apostles that they were to travel without purse or scrip (See Matt. 10: 9-10).

Peter and his fellow apostles thought that our Lord was asking for weapons to defend himself from his enemies, replied: "Lord, behold, here are two swords." To this comment, Jesus answered, "It is enough."

FROM THE GOSPEL OF MATTHEW AND MARK
(Matt. 26: 31-35; Mark 14: 27-32; JST Mark 14: 33)

Matthew states: "And when they had sung an hymn, they went out into the Mount of Olives." The Joseph Smith Translation of Mark says: "And now they [the eleven apostles] were grieved, and wept over him [Jesus]. And when they had sung a hymn, they went out into the Mount of Olives."

Therefore, Jesus and the eleven apostles left the upper room following the Feast of the Passover and walked a short distance to the Mount of Olives. While there, as Matthew has written, Jesus told them, "All ye shall be offended because of me this night . . . ." Peter, the dynamic man of action and faith, valiantly answered our Lord: "Though all men shall be offended because of thee, yet will I never be offended." The Joseph Smith Translation of Mark says: "Although all men

194

shall be offended with thee, yet I will never be offended."

Jesus stated: "Verily I say unto thee, That this day, even in this night, before the cock crow twice, thou shalt deny me thrice."

Not stunned by this surprising announcement, Mark informs us that Peter spoke more "vehemently" and declared: "If I should die with thee, I will not deny thee in any wise." Matthew wrote: "Though I should die with thee, yet will I not deny thee."

Not only did Peter make this declarative statement, but as Matthew and Mark have written: "Likewise also said all the disciples." Thus ends the recorded conversation between our Lord and his senior apostle. From what was spoken by our Lord, Peter's professed allegiance was fully tested that evening.

Chapter Thirty-Two

PETER, JAMES, AND JOHN IN GETHSEMANE
(Matt. 26: 36-46; Mark 14: 32-42; JST Mark 14: 36-37; Luke 22: 40-46; John 18: 1-2)

Following the conversation between Peter and our Lord, John says: "When Jesus had spoken these words, he went forth with his disciples over the brook Cedron, where was a garden, into the which he entered, and his disciples." Then, these explanatory words were written: "And Judas also, which betrayed him, knew the place: for Jesus ofttimes resorted thither with his disciples."

Regarding this garden, Elder Talmage has written this description: "Jesus and the eleven apostles went forth from the house in which they had eaten, passed through the city gate, which was usually left open at night during a public festival, crossed the ravine of the Cedron, or more accurately Kidron, brook, and entered an olive orchard known as Gethsemane, on the slope of Mount Olivet." Then, in an endnote, he says: "The name [Gethsemane] means 'oil-press' and probably has reference to a mill maintained at the place for the extraction of oil from the olives there cultivated. John refers to the spot as a garden, from which designation we may regard it as an enclosed space of private ownership . . . ."[205]

Surprisingly, we read these disheartening words as written in the Joseph Smith Translation of Mark: "And they [Jesus and the eleven apostles] came to a place which was named Gethsemane, which was a garden; and the disciples began to be sore amazed, and to be very heavy [in thought], and to complain in their hearts, wondering if this [Jesus] be the Messiah."

These eleven men had spent thousands of hours with our Lord; each of them had gained a testimony that Jesus was the Son of God; these noble men had seen Jesus perform countless number of miracles; why then, on the eve of his betrayal, did Peter and his fellow apostles wonder if Jesus was the Messiah? Though no definitive answer can be given, we may suppose that Satan was earnestly striving to raise doubts in the minds of those special witnesses of the Lord. And, like the explanation that was written in the previous chapter regarding Peter, those chosen men were not yet fully converted; they had not yet become a new creature by the power of the Holy Ghost. Whatever was their reasoning, Mark says: "And Jesus knowing their hearts, said to [eight of] his disciples, Sit ye here, while I shall pray." According to Luke's gospel, he further instructed them: "Pray that ye enter not into temptation."

PETER, JAMES, AND JOHN REBUKED BY JESUS
(JST Mark 14: 36-38, 40, 42-43, 47; Matt. 26: 38-39; Mark 14: 35; Luke 22: 41)

As was the case with the raising of the daughter of Jairus, and on the Mount of Transfiguration, we find out that Jesus took Peter, James, and John farther into the garden. As they walked, as written in the Joseph Smith Translation of Mark, our Lord "rebuked them"—apparently due to the doubts that arose in their hearts that he was the Messiah. We may suppose that these presiding apostles were greatly humbled and embarrassed over their thoughts. Jesus then told these three: "My soul is exceeding sorrowful, even unto death; tarry ye here and watch."

Matthew wrote that Jesus "went a little farther, and fell on his face, and prayed." Mark states that our Lord "went forward a little, and fell on the ground [prostrated himself], and prayed." Luke explains that he withdrew from the three apostles "about a stone's cast, and kneeled down, and prayed." Evidently, our Savior did each of these things during the course of repeated prayers on that agonizing night.

THE EVENTS THAT TRANSPIRED THAT EVENING
(Matt. 26: 39; JST Mark 14: 40-46; Luke 22: 42)

We cannot with surety reconstruct the events that transpired in the Garden of Gethsemane that evening. From what has been written by the gospel writers, we may safely believe that our Lord, in company with Peter, James, and John, spent several hours in this sacred place. While Jesus was praying, Peter, James, and John stopped watching and fell asleep.

However, before they slept, one or all heard a portion of the prayer offered by our Lord. Matthew says: "O my Father, if it be possible, let this cup pass from me: nevertheless not as I will, but as thou wilt."

The Joseph Smith Translation of Mark reads: "Abba, Father, all things are possible unto thee; take away this cup from me; nevertheless, not my will, but thine be done."

Luke's version: "Father, if thou be willing, remove this cup from me: nevertheless not my will, but thine, be done."

We further learn from Luke that "there appeared an angel unto him from heaven, strengthening him." From this information, we can safely believe that Peter, James, and John saw this heavenly visitant and informed Luke. Regarding this angel, Elder McConkie has written these thought-provoking words: "The angelic ministrant is not named . . . and if we might indulge in speculation, we would suggest that the angel who came into this second Eden [which is the Garden of Gethsemane] was the same person who dwelt in the first Eden [Garden of Eden]. At least Adam, who is Michael, the archangel—the head of the whole heavenly hierarchy of angelic ministrants—seems the logical one to give aid and comfort to his Lord on such a solemn occasion. Adam fell, and Christ redeemed men from the fall; theirs was a joint enterprise, both parts of which were essential for the salvation of the Father's children."[206]

Continuing with the Joseph Smith Translation of Luke, we read: "And being in an agony, he prayed more earnestly; and he sweat as it were great drops of blood falling down to the ground." Regarding our Lord's redemptive suffering, we use the words written in the *Book of Mormon*, as revealed by an angel to King Benjamin: "And lo, he shall suffer temptations, and pain of body . . . even more than man can suffer, except it be unto death; for behold, blood cometh from every pore, so great shall be his anguish for the wickedness and the abominations of his people" (See Mosiah 3: 7).

"And when he rose up from [this agonizing] prayer," says Luke, "and was come to his [three] disciples, he found them sleeping; for they were filled with sorrow."

WHY DID PETER, JAMES, AND JOHN SLEEP?
(JST Matt. 26: 37-38, 43; JST Mark 14: 41-47; JST Luke 22: 45-46)

Perhaps there are three reasons why Peter, James, and John fell asleep. First: Certain individuals deal with stress by sleeping. We may suppose that due to the stress they were experiencing over the pending death of their Lord, and being "filled with sorrow," those presiding apostles slept. Secondly: Just as it happened on the Mount of Transfiguration, so it happened in the Garden of Gethsemane, due to the late hour of the night, it was natural for those three apostles to be tired and they slept. Thirdly: "There is no mystery to compare with the mystery of redemption," as Elder McConkie explains, "not even the mystery of creation. Finite minds can no more comprehend how and in what manner Jesus performed his redeeming labors than they can comprehend how matter came into being, or how Gods began to be. Perhaps the very reason Peter, James, and John slept was to enable a divine providence to withhold from their ears, and seal up from their eyes, those things which only Gods can comprehend."[207]

From the Joseph Smith Translation of Matthew, we read what Jesus said to "Peter," when he found the three sleeping: "What, could ye not watch with me one hour? Watch and pray that ye enter not into temptation; the spirit indeed is willing; but the flesh is weak."

From the Joseph Smith Translation of Mark: "Simon, sleepest thou? Couldest [sic] not thou watch one hour? Watch ye and pray, lest ye enter into temptation."

Note: Instead of Jesus saying it, we read: "And they said unto him, The spirit truly is ready, but the flesh is weak."

From the Joseph Smith Translation of Luke: "Why sleep ye? rise and pray, lest ye enter into temptation."

Then, from the Joseph Smith Translation of Mark: "And again he went away and prayed, and spake the same words. And when he returned, he found them asleep again, for their eyes were heavy; neither knew they [Peter, James, and John] what to answer him."

"And he cometh to them the third time, and said unto them, Sleep on now and take rest; it is enough, the hour is come; behold, the Son of Man is betrayed into the hands of sinners. And after they had finished their sleep, he said, Rise up, let us go; lo, he who betrayeth me is at hand."

From the Joseph Smith Translation of Matthew: "And after they had slept, he said unto them, Arise, and let us be going. Behold, he is at hand that doth betray me."

This is all that is written of our Lord's atoning suffering in Gethsemane, and his conversations with his apostles. Regarding what the presiding apostles witnessed that evening, Elder Talmage has written these meaningful words:

"Peter had had a glimpse of the darksome road which he had professed himself so ready to tread; and the brothers James and John knew now better than before how unprepared they were to drink of the cup which the Lord would drain to its dregs."[208]

Chapter Thirty-Three

PETER CUT OFF THE RIGHT
EAR OF MALCHUS
(Matt. 26: 47-56; Mark 14: 43-52; Luke 22: 47-53;
John 18: 3-11)

While Jesus was speaking to the eleven apostles near the
entrance of the garden of Gethsemane, Judas approached with
a "great multitude" of people who had been sent by the Jewish
rulers. Carrying "lanterns and torches and weapons," this band
of men included military officers and religious leaders.
Paraphrasing the words of Edersheim, we find out that this
armed band or cohort was a detachment from the Roman
garrison of Antonia, consisting of between four to six hundred
men. These soldiers were kept on alert to quell disturbances
during the time of the Passover. The commander of this group
would not have sent a strong detachment without the prior
approval of the Roman procurator, Pontius Pilate. This also
explains the preparedness of Pilate to sit in judgment of our
Lord early the next morning.[209]

Besides the Roman soldiers, there were servants of the
chief priests, and many elders and Pharisees and temple
guards with their officers. Therefore, Judas led a "great multitude" of people—perhaps amounting to eight hundred to a
thousand men—who came that night to arrest one man who
testified that he was the Son of God.

We wonder what type of thoughts passed through Peter's
mind upon seeing Judas Iscariot leading this vast number of
armed men. Whatever those thoughts were, the senior apostle
understood why Judas had left the Passover meal in haste.

JESUS BETRAYED WITH A KISS

Prior to this multitude coming to the garden that night, the betrayer told them, "Whomsoever I shall kiss, that same is he; take him, and lead him away safely." Luke's version states that Judas "drew near unto Jesus, to kiss him. But Jesus said unto him, Judas, betrayest thou the Son of Man with a kiss?" Matthew's version says: "And forthwith he came to Jesus, and said, Hail, master; and kissed him. And Jesus said unto him, Friend, wherefore art thou come?" Mark's version reads that Judas "goeth straightway to him, and saith, Master, master; and kissed him."

"WHOM SEEK YE?"

After Judas had made the identification, as John has written, our Lord stepped forward and calmly asked, "Whom seek ye?" They answered, "Jesus of Nazareth." Again, our Lord responded, "I am he." Upon hearing this declaration the arresting soldiers, who had many times before arrested criminals and faced armed foes without hesitation or fear, "went backward, and fell to the ground." The reason: "The simple dignity and gently yet compelling force of Christ's presence," as Elder Talmage has written, "proved more potent than strong arms and weapons of violence."[210]

Again our Lord asked the multitude, "Whom seek ye." After composing themselves, they replied, "Jesus of Nazareth." With authority, Jesus said, "I have told you that I am he: if therefore ye seek me, let these go their way." This "last remark had reference to the apostles," Elder Talmage again says, "who were in danger of arrest; and in this evidence of Christ's solicitude for their personal safety, John saw a fulfillment of the Lord's then recent utterance in prayer, 'Of them which thou gavest me have

I lost none' (See John 18: 9). It is possible that had any of the Eleven been apprehended with Jesus and made to share the cruel abuse and torturing humiliation of the next few hours, their faith might have failed them, relatively immature and untried as it then was; even as in succeeding years many who took upon themselves the name of Christ yielded to persecution and went into apostasy."[211]

As Mark has written, the arresting soldiers approached our Lord and "they laid their hands on him, and took him." Jesus willingly consented to his arrest; he permitted himself to be bound as a common criminal. All the armies of the world could not have taken Jesus into custody unless he willed it. To illustrate this point, we recall that some time back our Lord had preached in a synagogue, and the people were angered with his words and they took Jesus to the brow of a hill that they might cast him over it, but passing through them, our Lord went his way (See Luke 4: 29-30). One of the reasons Jesus allowed his arrest was that while on the Mount of Transfiguration, he and Moses and Elijah "spake of his death, and also his resurrection, which he should accomplish at Jerusalem" (See JST Luke 9: 30-31).

PETER'S DEFENDING BEHAVIOR CAME FULLY ALIVE

Though there were a great multitude of armed men present, some of the apostles were ready to fight and die for their Master and they boldly asked, "Lord, shall we smite with the sword?" Immediately, the defending behavior of Peter came fully alive. Not waiting for a reply, this mighty man of action drew his sword and cut off the right ear of Malchus, a servant of the high priest. Some have written that this was a poorly aimed stroke by the senior apostle; however, we may safely believe that divine providence prevented Peter from taking the life of this man. If the senior apostle had taken the life of the servant, the multitude surely would have taken the life of Peter.

From the Joseph Smith Translation of Mark, we learn what our Lord said to Simon Peter: "He who taketh the sword shall perish with the sword." From the Joseph Smith Translation of Matthew: "Put up again thy sword into its place; for all they that take the sword shall perish with the sword. Thinkest thou that I cannot now pray to my Father, and he shall presently give me more than twelve legions of angels? But how then shall the Scriptures be fulfilled, that thus it must be?" John's version reads: "Put up thy sword into the sheath: the cup which my Father hath give me, shall I not drink it?"

To cure the injury caused by the senior apostle, and to demonstrate that he was the Son of God, our Lord asked liberty of the guards and "he put forth his finger and healed the servant of the high priest." We are left without knowledge of how this miracle affected the life of Malchus, or the people who witnessed it. Nor do we know how it affected Peter's thoughts and feelings. Notwithstanding, all of those individuals who were present witnessed this miraculous act performed by the man known as Jesus of Nazareth.

As a bound prisoner, our Lord "said unto the chief priests, and captains of the temple, and the elders," according to Mark's gospel, "Are ye come out, as against a thief with swords and with staves to take me? I was daily with you in the temple teaching, and ye took me not: but the scriptures must be fulfilled." Luke adds: "But this is your hour, and the power of darkness."

PETER AND HIS FELLOW APOSTLES FLED

The following is from the Joseph Smith Translation of Mark: "And the disciples, when they heard this saying, all forsook him and fled." This by no means demonstrates cowardice on their part, for Jesus had asked the multitude, "If therefore ye seek me, let these [my eleven apostles] go their way. That the saying might be fulfilled, which he spake, Of them which thou gavest me have I lost none" (See John 18: 8-9).

That the lives of the eleven apostles were in grave danger is shown from the description that a "certain young man, a disciple, having a linen cloth cast about his naked body," whom the soldiers tried to arrest; but this young man—who some scholars believe was John Mark—"left the linen cloth and fled from them naked, and saved himself out of their hands."

Chapter Thirty-Four

PETER DENIED KNOWING JESUS

PETER AND JOHN FOLLOWED JESUS TO THE PALACE
(Matt. 26: 57-75; Mark 14: 53-72; Luke 22: 54, 55-65; John
18: 15-18, 24-27)

After Jesus was led away captive from Gethsemane—this
sacred place, wherein our Savior had agonizingly atoned for
our sins—he was taken to the palace of Annas, an evil and adul-
terous Jew. This man was one of the wealthiest and most
influential Jews of his day. From the gospel writers, we are
further informed that Jesus was then taken to Caiaphas, the
son-in-law of Annas; from there, Jesus was taken to Pilate, the
Roman governor; Jesus was then taken to Herod, tetrarch of
Galilee and Perea; finally, Jesus was taken back to Pilate. Much
has been written of the false and blasphemous travesties that
were inflicted on our beloved Lord that remaining night and
early the next morning. For the purposes of this work, we will
only focus on the events that transpired in the life of Peter after
he and his fellow apostles fled for their lives.

We notably learn from Mark, "Peter followed him [our
Lord] afar off, even into the palace of the high priest: and he sat
with the servants, and warmed himself at the fire." According
to John's record, he and Peter regained their courage, and at a
safe distance, they followed Jesus and the soldiers to the
palace. Though we have no record of these two apostles being
present when Annas questioned Jesus, we know from the

scriptural record that John, due to his acquaintance with Caiaphas, and apparently his servants, was given permission to enter the residence of the high priest. "But Peter stood at the door without," not able to gain admittance. To help the senior apostle gain entrance, John spoke to the female servant who was tending the door; accordingly, Peter was allowed to enter. Whether by choice or by instruction, Peter remained in the hall or courtyard of the palace. John hurried to where our Lord was being arraigned before Caiaphas and the Sanhedrin.

PETER'S FIRST DENIAL

As Luke has written, "And when they had kindled a fire in the midst of the hall, and were set down together, Peter sat down among them." Then, from John, we learn that "the damsel" who had admitted him through the door, spoke aloud, "Art not thou also one of this man's disciples?"

Peter was no coward, and many times before as we have observed, spoke before properly thinking. Whether at this time the senior apostle spoke before thinking, or was purposely trying to conceal his identity in hope that he might some way rescue his beloved Master, he said, "I am not."

Not persuaded by his denial, as Matthew explains, she said: "Thou also wast with Jesus of Galilee." Mark says: "And thou also wast with Jesus of Nazareth."

Using deceptive words, Peter replied, "I know not, neither understand I what thou sayest."

To the other servants who were present, as Luke has written, this same "maid" exclaimed: "This man was also with him."

The senior apostle remarked: "Woman, I know him not."

"Peter was restless," as Elder Talmage has written, "his conscience and the fear of identification as one of the Lord's disciples troubled him. He left the crowd and sought partial seclusion in the porch."²¹² As Mark explains, when Peter went out into the porch, "the cock crew."

PETER'S SECOND DENIAL

While Peter was on the porch, as Matthew says, "another maid saw him, and said unto them that were there, This fellow was also with Jesus of Nazareth."

This time, the senior apostle "denied with an oath," saying, "I do not know the man."

A short time later, as Luke has written, a man said, "Thou art also of them."

Peter said, "Man, I am not." As has been written by various scholars, this conversation is classified as the second denial.

PETER'S THIRD DENIAL

Combining the words of Luke and John, we find out that "about the space of one hour" Peter left the porch, and stood by the fire, warming himself with others, "for it was cold." Some of those who stood by the fire said to the senior apostle, as Matthew says: "Surely thou also art one of them; for thy speech [betrayeth] thee." As Mark has it: "Surely thou art one of them: for thou art a Galilean. And thy speech agreeth thereto." As Luke says: "Of a truth this fellow also was with him: for he is a Galilean." As John has it: "Art not thou also one of his disciples?"

Peter answered: "I am not."

Then, one of the "servants of the high priest," who was a "kinsman"—meaning a relative—of Malchus, "whose ear Peter cut off," asked, "Did not I see thee in the garden with him?"

To these comments and questions, as Matthew says, Peter

began to "curse and to swear, saying, I know not the man." These were not vulgar words, or words of profanity, but words as a solemn oath. As Mark has it: "I know not this man of whom ye speak." Luke says: "Man, I know not what thou sayest." This is classified as the third denial. "And immediately," for the second time, "while he yet spake, the cock crew."

PETER WEPT BITTERLY

As Luke says, "the Lord turned, and looked upon Peter." Then, from the Joseph Smith Translation of Mark, "Peter called to mind the words which Jesus said unto him, Before the cock crow twice, thou shalt deny me thrice. And he went out, and fell upon his face, and wept bitterly."

WHY PETER DENIED KNOWING JESUS

As to the reasons why Peter denied knowing our Lord, no definitive answer can be given. Of the Twelve Apostles present when Jesus was arrested, only Peter drew his sword to defend his beloved Lord. Only the senior apostle and John dared to enter the palace where Christ was being arraigned before Caiaphas. And, only Peter verbally denied knowing Jesus.

One scholar has written that Peter, at this particular time, was a weak apostle. Another has written that Peter failed on this occasion to testify as one who was called to be a special witness of our Lord. Yet, another has written that Peter's denial was rather a failure to stand up and testify of the divinity of our Lord, as he had previously done on other notable occasions. President Joseph F. Smith, who then was second counselor to President Wilford Woodruff, has written these meaningful words: "Peter denied the Lord, and cursed and swore in order to make unbelievers think he was not a follower of Christ. He lied in the presence of God and before the world, and declared that he was not one of the disciples of Jesus. Did he commit the unpardonable sin? Was he a son of perdition? No; it was only the weakness of human nature that was in him, and he repented of it, repented sorely, and God forgave him. Afterwards he received the Holy Ghost, and he never committed any such sin again."[213]

As it pertains to the Saints in our day, who have received the Holy Ghost, many members—and especially after listening to General Conference—verbally profess to change their lives and be more faithful. Then, several weeks or months later, those same members have full knowledge that they have not been as faithful as they had verbally professed.

Peter had verbally professed to our Lord, "Though all men shall be offended because of thee, yet will I never be offended" (See Matt. 26: 33). Then, while in the palace of Caiaphas, he had full knowledge that he had not been as faithful as he had verbally professed. Though more noticeable, was Peter's profession different from those professions which are spoken by members of the Church in our day?

The senior apostle's triple denial of knowing Jesus was the result of many influences during that difficult and trying time. Therefore, we may safely conclude—as President Joseph F. Smith has well-written—that Peter's denial "was only the weakness of human nature that was in him, and he repented of it, repented sorely, and God forgave him."

Chapter Thirty-Five

PETER WAS TOLD: "FEED MY SHEEP"

PETER EXPLAINED HOW JUDAS DIED
(Matt. 27: 3-10; JST Matt. 27: 6; Acts 1: 13-18)

The gospel writers do not inform us when Judas Iscariot took his own life. Most gospel scholars believe that it happened before Jesus was crucified. The King James Version of Matthew says that Judas "went and hanged himself." At a formal Church meeting, the senior apostle provided additional information about the betrayer's death. After our Lord ascended into heaven, Peter and his fellow apostles met in a certain "upper room," with other disciples, including Mary, the mother of Jesus, some of her sons, and the little sisterhood of faithful women who had ministered to Jesus in Galilee. They met for the purpose of choosing a new apostle, due to the suicide of Judas. "Peter stood up" and told the congregation:

"Men and brethren, this scripture must needs have been fulfilled, which the Holy Ghost by the mouth of David spake before concerning Judas, which was guide to them [the multitude of armed men] that took Jesus. For he [Judas] was numbered with us [as one of the Twelve], and had obtained part of this ministry. Now this man [meaning: the chief priests] purchased a [potter's] field with the reward of iniquity [thirty pieces of silver]; and falling headlong, he [Judas] burst

asunder in the midst, and all his bowels gushed out . . .
Let his habitation be desolate, [his burial field] and let
no man dwell therein: and his bishoprick [apostolic
office] let another take."

From the Joseph Smith Translation of Matthew, we learn
that Judas "cast down the pieces of silver in the temple, and
departed, and went, and hanged himself on a tree. And
straightway he fell down, and his bowels gushed out, and he
died." Thus clarifying the words written by the King James
Version of Matthew, and the words spoken by Peter to the
congregation.

WAS PETER PRESENT WHEN JESUS DIED?
(Luke 23: 48-49; JST Luke 50)

No mention is made of Peter and his fellow apostles being
present at the crucifixion of our Lord, excepting John, who was
entrusted the care of Jesus' mother, Mary (See John 19: 25-26)
(See also the author's book, *Mary, Mother of Jesus*, p. 144).
However, it is interesting to note that when "all the people who
came together to that sight [the crucifixion of our Lord],
beholding the things which were done [the death of Jesus],
smote their breasts, and returned [to their homes]. And all his
acquaintance, and the women who followed him from Galilee,
stood afar off, beholding these things."

The phrase, "And all his acquaintance" means that all of
Jesus' friends were there. Therefore, we may properly believe
that Peter and his fellow apostles were standing "afar off,
beholding [those] things," excepting Judas who had already
committed suicide.

216

THE MONTH, DAY, AND YEAR JESUS DIED

Regarding the month, day, and year Jesus died, Elder Orson Pratt says: "We have already brought the testimony of chronologists to prove that he was crucified on Friday, the 6th of April" (As written in *Millennial Star* 28: 810, dated December 22, 1866). Then, in an address delivered in the Tabernacle, in Salt Lake City, Utah, on April 10, 1870, he said: "We find [from the *Book of Mormon*] that the ancient Israelites on this continent had a sign given of the exact time of the crucifixion and a revelation of the exact time of the Savior's birth, and according to their reckoning, they made him thirty-three years and a little over three days old from the time of his birth to the time that he hung upon the cross" (As recorded in *Journal of Discourses*, Volume 13, pages 126-127).

Lastly, from the Prophet Joseph Smith: "On the 6th of April [1833] . . . it being just 1800 years since the Savior laid down his life . . ." (*Documentary History of the Church* 1: 336-337, dated 6 April 1833).

Therefore, from these words spoken by early General Authorities, it appears evident that Jesus died Friday, April 6, A.D. 33.

PETER AND JOHN FOUND AN EMPTY TOMB
(Matt. 28: Mark 16; Luke 24; John 20; JST 20: 1)

It was Sunday, April 8, A.D. 33, the "first day of the week," and the third day following Jesus' death and burial. "At the earliest indication of dawn," as Elder Talmage has explained:

"The devoted Mary Magdalene and other faithful women set out for the tomb, bearing spices and ointments which they had prepared for the further anointing of the body of Jesus . . . On the way as they sorrowfully conversed, they seemingly for the first time thought of the difficulty of entering the tomb. 'Who shall roll us away the stone from the door of the sepulcher?' they asked one of another . . . At the tomb they saw the angel, and were afraid; but he said unto them: 'Fear not ye: for I know that ye seek Jesus, which was crucified. He is not here: for he is risen, as he said. Come, see the place where the Lord lay. And go quickly, and tell his disciples that he is risen from the dead; and, behold, he goeth before you into Galilee; there shall ye see him: lo, I have told you.'

"The women, though favored by angelic visitation and assurance, left the place amazed and frightened. Mary Magdalene appears to have been the first to carry word to the disciples concerning the empty tomb."[214]

From the words spoken by Mary, Peter and John were fearful that someone had stolen the body of Jesus. Without hesitation, "they ran both together" to the tomb. John, who evidently was younger and swifter, "did outrun Peter, and came first to the sepulcher." He stooped down, "and looking in, saw the linen clothes lying" in the tomb; "yet went he not in."

Without hesitation, Simon Peter—the dynamic man of action; the great defending champion of our Lord—rushed into the sepulcher. John then entered. Together they saw the grave clothes, and "the napkin, that was about his [Jesus'] head, not lying with the linen clothes, but wrapped together in a place by itself." After seeing the burial clothes that the resurrected body of our Lord went through, John wrote that he "believed." Then, giving explanation about himself and his fellow apostles: "For as yet they knew not the scripture, that he must rise again from the dead." That is, they had not known before, but they now knew that Christ was risen from the dead.

After seeing the burial clothes in the empty tomb, as Luke explains, Peter "departed, wondering in himself at that which was come to pass." John wrote: "Then the disciples [Peter and John] went away again unto their own home." Though Luke wrote that the senior apostle wondered at what he had just witnessed in the sepulcher, we may conclude that Peter—as did John—"believed" that Jesus was indeed risen the dead. His "wondering" would be comparable to "marveling" over the resurrection of his beloved Lord.

PETER SAW THE RESURRECTED LORD
(Luke 24: 33-35; 1 Cor. 15: 5)

As Elder McConkie has well-written: "It must needs be that he [Jesus] appear to Peter—to Peter the rock; to Peter the seer; to Peter the chief apostle; to Peter to whom he has already given the keys of his earthly kingdom. Peter must now step forward and preside and govern during the absence of his Lord."[215]

Though we do not know when or where this appearance occurred, we know that our Lord appeared to the senior apostle. From Luke, we find out that when the "eleven" apostles were gathered together,—meaning: Peter was present—with other members in a formal Church meeting. The apostolic testimony was born: "The Lord is risen indeed, and hath appeared to Simon."

Then, Paul says: "That Christ died for our sins . . . And that he was buried, and that he rose again the third day according to the scriptures: And that he was seen of Cephas, then of the twelve." Regarding Paul using the name "Cephas," we recall that when Peter first met the Messiah, Jesus said: "Thou art Simon the son of Jona: thou shalt be called Cephas, which is by interpretation, A stone" (See John 1: 42).

Therefore, two New Testament testimonies are recorded that Simon Peter, the Rock and the Seer, saw the resurrected

Lord. Though we do not know what was spoken at this private appearance, we may be assured that our resurrected Lord spoke words of comfort and counsel and direction to his senior apostle.

PETER WAS PRESENT WHEN THE RESURRECTED LORD APPEARED TWICE
(See Matt. 27: 3-5; Luke 24: 37-39; John 20: 24, 26-29)

Peter was present when the resurrected Christ first appeared in the upper room to a number of faithful members, including ten of the Twelve Apostles. The reason only ten apostles were present is as follows (1) Judas Iscariot had committed suicide. (2) For some unexplained reason, Thomas was not present. With the doors closed and locked, "Jesus himself stood in the midst of them. These apostolic witnesses "were terrified and affrighted, and supposed that they had seen a spirit." Jesus spoke these assuring words, "Why are ye troubled? And why do thoughts arise in your hearts? Behold my hands and my feet, that it is I myself: handle me, and see; for a spirit hath not flesh and bones, as ye see me have." A week later, Thomas was present with the ten apostles, meaning Peter was present, who had previously seen the risen Lord. Again, the Savior appeared and commanded his doubting apostle to "Reach hither thy finger, and behold my hands; and reach hither thy hand, and thrust it into my side: and be not faithless, but believing." After obeying, Thomas no longer doubted that Jesus was resurrected and had a tangible body of flesh and bones.

To this point in time, the senior apostle was blessed three times to see and hear the resurrected Christ. We now turn our attention to the fourth appearance of our Lord to Peter.

PETER WENT FISHING
(John 21: 1-24)

After our Lord was risen from the dead, Peter and his fellow apostles were given two commandments: One, to go to "Galilee" and meet Jesus on "a mountain" according to a prior "appointment" (See Matt. 28: 16). Secondly, "but tarry ye in the city of Jerusalem, until ye be endued [endowed] with power from on high" (See Luke 24: 49). Their appointment to meet the Lord on the mountain was a definite command where more than five hundred brethren had also been invited (See 1 Cor. 15: 6). As the apostles waited for that day to come, Simon Peter said: "I go a fishing." Six of the eleven apostles present with the senior apostle were: Thomas, Nathanael, James, John, and two who are not named. Some scholars believe these two were Andrew, and Philip, who had earlier been engaged with the senior apostle and others in the fishing trade. Desiring to be with their leader, they answered Peter: "We also go with thee."

Without delay, they went forth and entered into a ship. Though Peter and his fellow apostles had fished all night on the Sea of Galilee—known also as the Sea of Tiberias and as the Lake of Gennesaret—they had caught nothing. When morning came, "Jesus stood on the shore: but the disciples knew not that it was Jesus." He called out: "Children, have ye any meat [fish]?" "The noun of address, 'Children' is equivalent," as Elder Talmage says, "to our modern use of 'Sirs,' 'Men' or Lads.'"[216] The apostles truthfully answered: "No." Jesus replied: "Cast the net on the right side of the ship, and ye shall find." Obediently, they cast the net and "they were not able to draw it for the multitude of fishes."

PETER SWAM TO SHORE

John, who seemed to be more spiritually attuned, said unto Peter, "It is the Lord." Simon Peter, who was naked—probably because he was changing his dirty fishing clothes to cleaner ones—hurried and "girt his fisher's coat unto him," and jumped from the ship and swam to the shore to meet the resurrected Lord. The other apostles left the larger fishing ship and entered a small boat in which they rowed to shore, "dragging the net with fishes."

When those in the small boat came to shore, "they saw a fire of coals there, and fish laid thereon, and bread." Jesus told them: "Bring of the fish which ye have now caught."

Simon Peter quickly waded into the shallow water, "and drew the net to land full of great fishes." For some reason, the fish were counted and they amounted to "a hundred and fifty three" great fishes. The narrator is careful to mention: "And for all there were so many, yet was not the net broke." John says this was "the third time that Jesus shewed himself to his disciples," as a group, "after that he was risen from the dead." However, as we have discovered, this was the fourth appearance of our Lord to Peter.

The Lord politely said to his apostles: "Come and dine." John explains that none of the apostles dared asked him, "Who art thou?" because they knew it was the Lord. Then, Jesus gave the apostles bread and fish to eat. Though the account does not mention it, we may properly assume that our Lord also ate the prepared meal that memorable morning; proving once again to Peter and his fellow apostles that Jesus had a tangible, resurrected body of flesh and bones.

PETER'S TRIPLE DECLARATION OF LOVE

When Jesus and his apostles "had dined," our Lord said to Simon Peter: "Simon, son of Jonas, lovest thou me more than these?" Perhaps our Lord pointed at the fish that had been caught; whatever transpired, Peter answered humbly: "Yea, Lord; thou knowest I love thee." Jesus said: "Feed my lambs."

A second time our Lord asked the senior apostle: "Simon, son of Jonas, lovest thou me?" Again, Peter answered: "Yea, Lord; Thou knowest that I love thee." To this comment, Jesus said: "Feed my sheep."

Then, for the third time, Jesus asked: "Simon, son of Jonas, lovest thou me?"

Peter, who was grieved at the repeated questions, responded firmly: "Lord, thou knowest all things; thou knowest that I love thee." Jesus said: "Feed my sheep."

"The commission 'Feed my sheep' was an assurance of the Lord's confidence," as Elder Talmage says, "and of the reality of Peter's presidency among the apostles."[217]

Peter had three times denied knowing Jesus; now, three times he had affirmed that he loved his beloved Lord. Jesus told Simon Peter—the designated President of His Church—to feed his sheep. How was that love to be shown? By the senior apostle faithfully serving his fellowmen.

PETER WAS TOLD OF HIS CRUCIFIXION

Still speaking to Peter, Jesus said: "When thou wast young, thou girdedst thyself, and walkedst whither thou wouldest: but when thou shalt be old, thou shalt stretch forth thy hands, and another shall gird thee, and carry thee wither thou wouldest not." Regarding this statement, John says: "This spake he [Jesus], signifying by what death he [Peter] should glorify God."

Simon Peter would be crucified, the same manner as our Lord had been crucified. The senior apostle's arms would be stretched forth upon the beams of the cross, the soldiers will gird him with a loincloth, and he would be carried where he would not want to go—to his death by crucifixion.

After speaking those words, Jesus said to Peter, "Follow me." As Elder Talmage says: "The command had both immediate and future significance. The man followed as Jesus drew apart from the others on the shore; yet a few years and Peter would follow his Lord to the cross."[218]

Regarding Peter's crucifixion, President Brigham Young said: "We are still further informed by historians that the Apostle Peter was crucified, head downwards."[219] Elder George Q. Cannon explained: "Peter was crucified at Rome with his head downwards, not considering himself worthy to be crucified as his Lord had been."[220] In conclusion, President George A. Smith, First Counselor to President Brigham Young, says: "It is said of this Apostle [Peter] that when he came to the end of his earthly career, which was crucifixion by the hands of his enemies, he requested that he might be crucified with his feet upwards; because he had denied his Master, he was unwilling to be put on the cross in the same position."[221]

PETER WAS TOLD OF JOHN'S TRANSLATION

As our Lord and the senior apostle walked together, Peter, "turning about," saw John—curious as to what would happen to his close colleague and friend— and asked Jesus: "Lord, and what shall this man do?"

Jesus answered, "If I will that he tarry till I come, what is that to thee?" He further told Peter: "Follow thou me." The beloved apostle also wrote: "Then went this saying abroad among the brethren, that [John] should not die."

John's own account of his translation was revealed to the Prophet Joseph Smith. As it pertains to our Savior's words to the senior apostle, we read: "And for this cause the Lord said unto Peter: If I will that he tarry till I come, what is that to thee? For he desired of me that he might bring souls unto me, but thou desiredst that thou mightest speedily come unto me in my kingdom. I say unto thee, Peter, this was a good desire; but my beloved has desired that he might do more, or a greater work yet among men than what he has before done." Then, regarding the three presiding apostles, the Lord further stated: "Yea, he [John] has undertaken a greater work; therefore I will make him as flaming fire and a ministering angel; he shall minister for those who shall be heirs of salvation who dwell on the earth. And I will make thee [Peter] to minister for him [John] and for [his] brother James; and unto you three I will give this power and the keys of this ministry until I come. Verily I say unto you [Peter], ye shall both [Peter and John] have according to your desires, for ye both joy in that which ye have desired" (See D&C 7: 4-8).

"That John still lives in the embodied state," explains Elder Talmage, "and shall remain in the flesh until the Lord's yet future advent, is attested by later revelation. In company with his martyred and resurrected companions, Peter and James, and the 'disciple whom Jesus loved' has officiated in the restoration of the Holy Apostleship in this the dispensation of the fulness of times."[222]

PETER, JAMES, AND JOHN IN THE FIRST PRESIDENCY
(John 20: 22; Mark 16: 19-20; Luke 24: 49-53; Acts 1-28)

After the apostles were endowed from on high, both by receiving sacred blessings that are generally given in holy places, and receiving the Holy Ghost on the day of Pentecost,

Peter served as the President of the Church, with his counselors, James and John. Whether or not they met for meetings separately from the other apostles, we are not informed.

Luke is the author of Acts. This book tells the story of the rise of Christ's Church under the direction of the apostles, following the resurrection of our Lord. Peter is the prominent Church leader in chapters one to eight and ten through twelve. In chapters nine and thirteen through twenty-eight, Paul is the prominent Church leader who took the gospel to the Gentile world.

A few scholars have explained that the first half of the book of Acts narrates Peter's ministry in Palestine, for twenty years, following our Lord's death and resurrection. During this time, Peter also preached in the city of Antioch and had a confrontation with Paul (See Gal. 2: 11-21). These same scholars believe that about 56 A.D., Peter was probably making regular missionary journeys, in company with his wife (See 1 Cor. 9: 5).

Briefly, the rest of this chapter will highlight events that transpired in Peter's life while he served as the President of the Church. Shortly after Jesus was resurrected and ascended into heaven, Peter conducted the meeting where Matthias was chosen as a new apostle to take the place of Judas Iscariot (See Acts 1: 15-26). Peter, speaking for the eleven apostles, declared the gospel in Jerusalem on the day of Pentecost (See Acts 2: 1-21). On that same day, three thousand new converts were baptized and came into the Church (See Acts 2: 41-47).

Peter, with John present, healed a man who was lame from birth (See Acts 3: 1-6). After Peter and John healed that man, five thousand men came into the fold, for "all men glorified God for that which was done" (See Acts 4: 1-22).

Peter and John boldly testified to the Jewish council that they would continue to preach of Christ (See Acts 4: 13-22). Later, the sick were laid in the street desiring that "at least the shadow of Peter, passing by" might heal them (See Acts 5: 12-16). At an unspecified time, Peter and his fellow apostles choose seven men to assist them in their ministry (See Acts 6: 1-6).

When the gospel was taken to Samaria, Peter and John went there to supervise the work, and together, they laid on hands for the gift of the Holy Ghost (See Acts 8: 14-17). Peter told the man Simon to repent for trying to buy the gift of the Holy Ghost (See Acts 8: 18-25). From a special request, Peter raised from the dead a woman named Dorcas (See Acts 9: 32-43). Peter received a vision regarding unclean beasts (See Acts 10: 9-20). Then, from this vision, Peter knew that the gospel should be taken to Cornelius and other gentiles (See Acts 10: 21-35). "While Peter yet spake these words, the Holy Ghost fell on them that heard the word." Here, God poured out the Holy Ghost upon Cornelius, his family, and his friends as a sign to Peter that the gospel was to be taken to the Gentiles (See Acts 10: 44-48).

PETER AND JAMES
(Acts 12: 1-19; 15: 6-21)

Repeating what has previously been written in chapter thirteen of this book, we learn what transpired approximately eleven years after Jesus was crucified: "Now about that time that Herod the king stretched forth his hands to vex certain [leaders] of the church. And he killed James the brother of John with the sword."

Tragically, one of Peter's counselors in the First Presidency had been slain. By reason that a vacancy occurred in the First Presidency, Peter, by inspiration, called James, the Lord's brother, to be his new counselor. Shortly after James the brother of John had been slain, Peter, himself, was put in prison. By divine intervention, an angel of the Lord freed Peter from his captors.

At the "house of Mary the mother of John, whose surname was Mark; where many were gathered together praying," Peter said to the people, "Go shew these things [explain what had just transpired] unto James, and to the brethren [who were the apostles]. And he departed, and went into another place."

After Paul was made an apostle, he explained: "Neither went I up to Jerusalem to them which were apostles before me; but I went into Arabia, and returned again unto Damascus. Then after three years I went up to Jerusalem to see Peter, and abode with him fifteen days. But other of the apostles saw I none, save James the Lord's brother" (See Gal. 1: 17-19).

PETER'S COUNSELORS IN THE FIRST PRESIDENCY

In the first half of Acts, John, the other counselor in the First Presidency, appears prominent with Peter. In the second half of Acts, James, the Lord's brother, appears to be the prominent leader at Jerusalem. He is mentioned several times in association with Peter.

PETER'S DEATH

Regarding Peter's death by crucifixion, the first Christian chronologies—whom some have termed it a tradition—has it that toward the close of his life, Peter visited Rome and suffered martyrdom there in the persecutions raised by Nero, about 67 A.D. Therefore, Peter, the President of the Church, died by crucifixion; James, the brother of John, died by the sword; and John, who was translated, never tasted death. With this understanding, we turn our attention to when Peter, James, and John appeared in 1829 to the Prophet Joseph Smith and Oliver Cowdery.

Chapter Thirty-Six

PETER, JAMES, AND JOHN
APPEARED IN 1829

JOHN THE BAPTIST CONFERRED
THE AARONIC PRIESTHOOD
(*History of the Church*, Vol. 1, p. 39-40; D&C 13)

In the spring of 1829, the Prophet Joseph Smith and his scribe, Oliver Cowdery, were translating the *Book of Mormon*. On May 15, 1829, they went to the woods to pray and inquire of the Lord—along the bank of the Susquehanna River, near Harmony, Pennsylvania—regarding baptism for the remission of sins, that they had found mentioned in the translation of the gold plates. While they were praying and calling upon the Lord for an answer, a heavenly messenger—who announced himself as John, the same that is called John the Baptist—descended in a cloud of light. This angel explained that he was acting under the direction of Peter, James, and John, the ancient apostles, who held the keys of the higher priesthood, which was called the Priesthood of Melchizedek. Then, this heavenly messenger laid his hands upon the heads of Joseph and Oliver and ordained them by saying: "Upon you my fellow servants, in the name of Messiah I confer the priesthood of Aaron, which holds the keys of the ministering of angels, and of the gospel of repentance, and of baptism by immersion for the remission of sins; and this shall never be taken again from the earth, until the sons of Levi do offer again an offering unto the Lord in righteousness."

John the Baptist told Joseph and Oliver that this Aaronic priesthood had not the power of the laying on of hands for the gift of the Holy Ghost, but that this priesthood should be conferred on them hereafter. This same messenger commanded Joseph Smith to baptized Oliver Cowdery, and afterwards that Oliver baptized Joseph. After their baptism, Joseph laid his hands upon the head of Oliver and ordained him to the Aaronic Priesthood. Then, Oliver laid his hands upon Joseph and ordained him to that same priesthood. The angel further told them that Joseph should be called the first elder of the Church, and that Oliver should be called the second.

PETER, JAMES, AND JOHN
CONFERRED THE MELCHIZEDEK PRIESTHOOD
(D&C 27: 12-13; 128: 20)

Though the exact date is not recorded, a short time after John the Baptist conferred the Aaronic Priesthood upon Joseph Smith and Oliver Cowdery, Peter, James, and John—the original First Presidency of the Church in the meridian of time—appeared to Joseph Smith and Oliver Cowdery and conferred the Melchizedek priesthood upon them. Regarding their appearance, the Lord told the Prophet Joseph Smith:

"Peter, and James, and John, whom I have sent unto you, by whom I have ordained you and confirmed you to be apostles, and especial witnesses of my name, and bear the keys of your ministry and of the same things which I revealed unto them.

Unto whom I have committed the keys of my kingdom, and a dispensation of the gospel for the last times; and for the fulness of times, in the which I will gather together in one all things, both which are in heaven, and which are on earth."

Concerning the appearance of these ancient members of the First Presidency, Joseph Smith testified: "Peter, James, and John [came] in the wilderness between Harmony, Susquehanna county, and Colesville, Broome county, on the Susquehanna river, declaring themselves as possessing the keys of the kingdom, and of the dispensation of the fulness of times!"

"What did these ancient apostles restore?" Elder McConkie asked and answered, "They brought back the Melchizedek Priesthood, which administers the gospel and governs the Church and includes the holy apostleship. They conferred the keys of the kingdom and the keys of the dispensation of the fulness of times. As a result, the Church was organized again among men on April 6, 1830. They restored the apostolic commission to go into all the world and preach the gospel with signs following those who believe."[223]

PETER WAS IN THE KIRTLAND TEMPLE

The following information is obtained from an address given by President Heber C. Kimball, First Counselor to President Brigham Young, regarding clothing: "Some of you [Latter-day Saints] have got an idea that wool will not do; but let me inform you that when Peter came and sat in the Temple in Kirtland, he had on a neat woolen garment, nicely adjusted round the neck."

Then, he provided this information about the garments of the Holy Priesthood: "To return to the subject of the garments of the Holy Priesthood, I will say that the one which Jesus had on when he appeared to the Prophet Joseph was neat and clean, and Peter had on the same kind, and he also had a key in his hand."

Regarding the messengers who restored priesthood keys, President Kimball explained: John [the Baptist] also came and administered unto Joseph Smith, and remember that Peter, James and John hold the keys pertaining to their dispensation and pertaining to this, and they came and conferred their Priesthood and authority upon Joseph the Seer, which is for the gathering together of all who seek the way of life."[224]

It is interesting to note that Peter—the Rock and the Seer—appeared to Joseph Smith, who is also designated "the Seer." Both of these mighty prophets had many things in common. To mention a few: Both were unlearned in the eyes of the world; both overcame weaknesses and rose to great spiritual heights; both became the president and prophet of Christ's Church after seeing the resurrected Lord; both were able to see ancient prophets; both bestowed priesthood and keys; both remained true and faithful to our Lord; and lastly, both met a martyr's death.

EACH OF US CAN BECOME LIKE PETER

In conclusion, from what has been written in this work, it is declared that Simon Peter was one of the greatest of men. This noble soul was a dynamic man of action, a man of faith, a man of God. And like Peter, each of us can overcome human weaknesses and rise to great spiritual heights.

Peter, My Brother

by President Spencer W. Kimball,

Acting President of the Quorum of the Twelve Apostles
© Intellectual Reserve, Inc. (Used by permission)

A speech given July 13, 1971 at Brigham Young University

Today I wish to talk about my brother, my colleague, my fellow apostle—Simon Barjona or Cephas or Peter the Rock.

Some time ago a newspaper in a distant town carried an Easter Sunday religious editorial by a minister who stated that the presiding authority of the early-day church fell because of self-confidence, indecision, evil companions, failure to pray, lack of humility, and fear of man. He then concluded:

> *Let us as people, especially those who are Christians and claim to abide by the Word of God, not make the same mistakes and fall as Peter fell.* (Rev. Dorsey E. Dent, "A Message for This Week.")

As I read this, I had some strange emotions. I was shocked, then I was chilled, then my blood changed its temperature and began to boil. I felt I was attacked viciously, for Peter was my brother, my colleague, my example, my prophet, and God's anointed. I whispered to myself, "That is not true. He is maligning my brother."

A Man with Vision

Then I opened my New Testament. I could find no such

233

character as this modern minister described. Instead, I found a man who had grown perfect through his experiences and sufferings—a man with vision, a man of revelations, a man fully trusted by his Lord Jesus Christ.

I remember his sad, triple denial of his acquaintance with the Lord in those terrifying, frustrating moments. I recall his tearful repentance. Many times he was rebuked by the Master, but he learned by experience and never seemed to make the same error twice. I see a lowly fisherman, untaught and untrained, climb gradually under the tutelage of the best Teacher to the high pinnacle of great faith, bold leadership, unwavering testimony, unparalleled courage, and almost limitless understanding. I see the lay disciple become the chief apostle to preside over the Lord's church and kingdom. I hear him breathing heavily as he laboriously climbs the steep Mount of Transfiguration. Here he sees and hears unspeakable things and has the transcendent experience of being in the presence of his God, Elohim; Jehovah, his Redeemer; and other heavenly beings.

His eyes had seen, his ears had heard, and his heart had understood and accepted the wondrous happenings of the days from the baptism of the Master in the waters of Jordan to the ascension of his Redeemer from the Mount of Olives.

I see this great church president assume leadership of the church. I see the sick and infirm arise and leap to health and normalcy. I hear his powerful sermons. I see him walk steadily, unflinchingly to martyrdom and drink of its bitter cup.

But this sectarian minister belittled him, unmercifully undercut him, and downgraded him.

Much of the criticism of Simon Peter is centered in his denial of his acquaintance with the Master. This has been labeled "cowardice." Are we sure of his motive in that recorded denial? He had already given up his occupation and placed all worldly goods on the altar for the cause. If we admit that he was cowardly and denied the Lord through timidity, we can still find a great lesson. Has anyone more completely overcome mortal selfishness and weakness? Has anyone repented more sincerely? Peter has been accused of being harsh, indiscreet, impetuous, and fearful. If all these were true, then we will still ask, Has any man ever more completely triumphed over his weaknesses?

The First Apostle

Good men were among the Lord's followers, yet Cephas was chosen the number one. The Lord knew well the guilelessness of Nathaniel, the tender love of John, the erudition of Nicodemus, and the faithfulness and devotion of James and other brethren. Christ knew men's inner thoughts and saw their manifestations of faith. In short, he knew men; yet he chose from all of them this great character who possessed the virtues, powers, and leadership needed to give stability to the church and to lead men to accept the gospel and follow truth.

When Christ chose this fisherman for his first and chief apostle, he was taking no chances. He picked a diamond in the rough—a diamond that would need to be cut, trimmed, and polished by correction, chastisement, and trials—but nevertheless a diamond of real quality. The Savior knew this apostle could be trusted to receive the keys of the kingdom, the sealing and the loosing power. Like other humans, Peter might make some errors in his developing process, but he would be solid, trustworthy, and dependable as a leader of the kingdom of God. Even with so perfect a teacher, it was difficult to learn the vast gospel plan in three years.

Peter inquired of Jesus:

Behold, we have forsaken all, and followed thee; what shall we have therefore?
And Jesus said unto them, Verily I say unto you,

*that ye which have followed me, in the regeneration
when the Son of man shall sit in the throne of his glory,
ye also shall sit upon twelve thrones, judging the twelve
tribes of Israel.* (Matthew 19:27-28.)

Is it conceivable that the omniscient Lord would give all
these powers and keys to one who was a failure or unworthy?

If Peter was cowardly, how brave he became in so short a
time. If he was weak and vacillating, how strong and positive he
became in weeks and months. If he was unkind, how tender and
sympathetic he became almost immediately. Responsibility as a
refiner and a purger usually takes time.

If Peter was frightened in the court when he denied his association with the Lord, how brave he was hours earlier when he
drew his sword against an overpowering enemy, the night mob.
Later defying the people and state and church officials, he boldly
charged, "Him [the Christ] . . . ye have taken, and by wicked
hands have crucified and slain." (Acts 2:23.) To the astounded
populace at the healing of the cripple at the Gate Beautiful, he
exclaimed, "Ye men of Israel . . . the God of our fathers, hath
glorified his Son Jesus; whom ye delivered up, and denied him
in the presence of Pilate . . . ye denied the Holy One . . . . And
killed the Prince of life, whom God hath raised from the dead;
whereof we are witnesses." (Acts 3:12-15.)

Does this portray cowardice? Quite a bold assertion for a
timid one. Remember that Peter never denied the divinity of
Christ. He only denied his association or acquaintance with the
Christ, which is quite a different matter.

Could it have been confusion and frustration that caused
Peter's denial? Could there still have been some lack of understanding concerning the total unfolding of the plan? Being a
leader, Peter was a special target of the adversary. As the Lord
said:

Simon, Simon, behold, Satan hath desired to have you, that he may sift you as wheat:
But I have prayed for thee that thy faith fail not.
(Luke 22:31-32.)

Peter was under fire; all the hosts of hell were against him. The die had been cast for the Savior's crucifixion. If Satan could destroy Simon now, what a victory he would score. Here was the greatest of all living men. Lucifer wanted to confuse him, frustrate him, limit his prestige, and totally destroy him. However, this was not to be, for he was chosen for and ordained to a high purpose in heaven, as was Abraham.

Peter followed the Savior to his trial and sat in the outer court. What else could he do? He knew that many times the Savior himself had escaped from the crowd by slipping out of their clutches. Would he again do so?

Though the Lord taught of the coming crucifixion and resurrection, neither Simon nor anyone else fully comprehended his meaning. Was this so strange? Never before had there been such a person or such an occurrence on the earth. Millions today cannot understand the resurrection, even though it has been preached for nineteen hundred years as a reality with many infallible proofs. Could these men, then, be criticized for not fully understanding this frustrating situation?

Is it possible that there might have been some other reason for Peter's triple denial? Could he have felt that circumstances justified expediency? When he bore a strong testimony in Caesarea Philippi, he had been told that "they should tell no man that he was Jesus the Christ." (Matthew 16:20.)

When the three apostles came down from the Mount of Transfiguration, they were again charged implicitly, "Tell the vision to no man, until the Son of man be risen again from the dead." (Matthew 17:9.) Could Peter have felt this was not the time to tell of Christ? He had been with his Lord in Nazareth when the Savior was taken by his own people to the brow of the hill, "whereon their city was built, that they might cast him down headlong. But he passing through the midst of them went his way." (Luke 4:29-30.) Surely Peter did not think of this escape as cowardice but as wise expediency. Christ's time was not come.

The Approaching Crucifixion

When the Lord had spent some energy in attempting to explain the coming crisis—"how that he must go unto Jerusalem, and suffer many things of the elders and chief priests and scribes, and be killed, and be raised again the third day"—Peter attempted to dissuade the Savior from thinking of such calamity. (See Matthew 16:21.) He was promptly chastised for suggesting escape from the tragedy. Perhaps he should have understood that it was the Lord's will that the dire happenings occur.

What this meant—that the hour was now come—Peter may not have fully realized, but he was prohibited from resisting that coming crucifixion by the Redeemer himself. Was he frustrated? Perhaps for the moment, but how many of us in a hostile camp, totally helpless to save, would champion the Lord under such circumstances, especially when previous efforts had been repulsed? Had not Peter single-handedly already raised his sword against a "great multitude with swords and staves"? (Matthew 26:47.) Had he not attempted to defend the Lord from all the mob's manhandling and kidnapping, and was he not stopped by his Lord?

The Savior had walked calmly from Gethsemane's garden, seemingly resigned to the inevitable sacrifice of himself. Simon had courageously manifested his willingness to alone fight the great mob to protect his Master. At the risk of death he had struck the contemptible Malchus and sliced off his ear. But this act of bravery and personal disregard was stopped by the Lord, who said to his loyal apostle:

> *Put up again thy sword into his place: for all they that take the sword shall perish with the sword.*
> *Thinkest thou that I cannot now pray to my Father, and he shall presently give me more than twelve legions of angels?* (Matthew 26:52-53.)

What more could Peter do? How else could he show his loyalty and courage? Could it be that in these last hours Peter realized that he should stop protecting his Lord, that the crucifixion was inevitable, and that regardless of all his acts, the Lord was moving toward his destiny? I do not know. I only know that this apostle was brave and fearless.

Events followed each other in rapid succession. At Gethsemane Peter was futilely trying to defend his Lord one hour; in the next he was following the mob. Apparently the Savior was voluntarily suffering men to heap monumental indignities upon him. What should Peter do?

He boldly and meaningfully postulated to the Savior, "Though all men shall be offended because of thee, yet will I never be offended." (Matthew 26:33.) To which the Lord replied, "This night, before the cock crow, thou shalt deny me thrice." (Matthew 26:34.)

This was a critical moment. Peter's act of protection with his sword-slashing had been after this prediction was made. He had tried. He had seen one apostle betray his Master with a kiss, and his Master had not repulsed him. Peter had been reminded that angels could be summoned if protection was needed; he had been commanded to put away his sword. Even now he did not desert his Master but followed sorrowfully behind the jeering crowd. He would remain to the end. He likely heard every accusation, saw every indignity heaped upon his Lord, felt all the injustice of the mock trial, and noted the perfidy of false witnesses perjuring their souls. He saw them foully expectorate in the face of the Holy One; he saw them buffet, strike, slap, and taunt him. He observed the Lord making no resistance, calling for no protective legions of angels, asking for no mercy. What was Peter to think now?

His Denial

A smart aleck damsel accused Peter, "Thou also wast with Jesus of Galilee."(Matthew 26:69.) What would his further defense of the Lord accomplish in this situation? Would it displease Jesus? Would it only destroy Peter himself without beneficial effect? Would Christ want him to fight now, when he had denied him that privilege earlier that evening?

Then another maid announced to the bystanders and villains, "This fellow was also with Jesus of Nazareth." (Matthew 26:71.) Peter replied, "I do not know the man." (Matthew 26:72.) And others, recognizing his Galilean accent, declared, "Surely thou also art one of them; for thy speech [betrayeth] thee." (Matthew 26:73.)

What was he to do? Could he do more? What would have been the result had he admitted his connection? Would he have lived to preside over the church? Peter had seen the Savior escape from crowds many times and hide from assassins. Is it conceivable that Peter also saw advisable advantage to the cause in his denial? Had Peter come to fully realize the hidden meaning in the oft-repeated phrase "Mine hour is not yet come" (John 2:4), and did he now understand that "now is the Son of man glorified" (John 13:31)?

I do not pretend to know what Peter's mental reactions were nor what compelled him to say what he did that terrible night. But in light of his proven bravery, courage, great devotion, and limitless love for the Master, could we not give him the benefit of the doubt and at least forgive him as his Savior seems to have done so fully. Almost immediately Christ elevated him to the highest position in his church and endowed him with the complete keys of that kingdom.

Simon Barjona did not have long to consider the matter or change his decisions, for he now heard the cock crow twice and was reminded of Christ's prediction. He was humbled to the dust. Hearing the bird's announcement of the dawn reminded him not only that he had denied the Lord but also that all the Lord had said would be fulfilled, even to the crucifixion. He went out and wept bitterly. Were his tears for personal repentance only, or were they mingled with sorrowful tears in realization of the fate of his Lord and Master and his own great loss?

Only hours passed until he was among the first at the tomb as the head of the group of believers. Only weeks passed until he was assembling the saints and organizing them into a compact, strong, and unified community. It was not long before he was languishing in prison, being beaten, abused, and "sifted as wheat" as Christ had predicted. (See Luke 22:31.)

Of Humble Origin

Simon Peter, son of Jonas, began his matchless career under most humble circumstances. A common operator of boats, a fisher of fish, and a man once rated as "ignorant and unlearned," he climbed the ladder of knowledge until he knew, as perhaps no other living person, his Father, Elohim; the Son, Jehovah; and Christ's program and relationship with men. He was spiritual and devout. He came without persuasion, probably walking every step of the length of the major Jordan to hear the powerful sermons of the fearless John the Baptist. Little did he know the great things in store for him. Here he heard the voice of the prophet and may have been baptized by him.

Peter's brother, Andrew, declared, "We have found the Messias, which is, being interpreted, the Christ." (John 1:41.) They had undoubtedly heard John the Baptist declare, "Behold the Lamb of God, which taketh away the sin of the world." (John 1:29.) But to hear the voice of the living Father, God, now acknowledge Jesus as his Begotten Son must have stirred this humble fisherman to his foundations.

Simon Peter was ill prepared at this time to assume great responsibility, but the Master knew his potential. On the day of his call began the intensive training that was to bring this humble man and his associates to great leadership, immortality, and eternal life.

Simon Peter's education, both secular and spiritual, had been limited, but now he followed the Master Teacher. He heard the Sermon on the Mount; he stood with the Redeemer in the boat and heard the masterful sermons to the congregated people. He sat in synagogues, listening to the convincing and powerful statements of the Creator. The Scriptures were unfolded as they traveled the dusty or rocky paths of Galilee. Surely, his innumerable questions were answered by the Lord as they ate together, slept together, and walked together. The hours were precious as rare jewels. He heard the parables given to the people and learned the rich lessons therein.

Peter heard the constant flow of divinity in the ceaseless unfolding of the way of life. He grasped many lessons readily but had difficulty in understanding the experiences that had never before occurred on earth. He perceived the darkening shadow and the lowering clouds but could not fully comprehend their meaning. No personage in his experience had ever given his life in this manner. No soul on earth had ever been resurrected. It took time for these awesome truths to penetrate his mind. It was hard for him to think of spiritual leadership only. Peter expected Christ to take the sword and redeem Israel. But when Gethsemane was passed, when Golgotha was a hard nightmare, when the Lord had risen and ascended, and when the Comforter had come, the great compelling truth burst forth and was impressed upon his mind. The miscellaneous tiles were now set into a beautiful pattern. The mosaic was a glorious reality; and Peter, James and John and their associates went forth to convert a hard, resisting world.

Peter was full of faith. He never faltered. From the day he forsook his nets and boats, his feet never turned away. Even in his moment of denial, he was as near to his Lord as he could be. Let him who would be critical of this apostle put himself in the same place—among the bitterest enemies, persecutors, and assassins—with a growing knowledge of the futility of defending his Lord, whose hour had come. He who had forgiven his crucifiers also forgave Peter who had denied him.

Peter was a man of faith. He healed the sick by their merely passing through his shadow. Prison walls could not hold him. Because of him, the dead came back to life. He walked upon the water. Though this was not a total triumph, has any other human soul succeeded? Let him who would scoff at Peter's momentary wavering try such a feat himself.

Simon Peter was humble. He recognized James and John, who were with him on the Holy Mount and who shared with him the sorrows of Gethsemane. Perhaps his first official act, as presiding authority, was to call a conference at which the saints were to have voice in filling the vacancy in the Quorum of the Twelve. A new witness was chosen.

When the lame walked under the administration of Peter and John and when the awestricken multitude gaped and wondered, Peter gave credit to the God of Israel, saying, "Why look ye so earnestly on us, as though by our power or holiness we had made this man to walk?" (Acts 3:12.) When Dorcas Tabitha lay dead, there was no display nor ostentation. He simply "put them all forth, and kneeled down, and prayed," and presented the living Tabitha back to her friends. (See Acts 9:40-41.)

He accepted threats, beatings, and calumny. He defied those who condemned his Lord, saying, "We ought to obey God rather than men." (Acts 5:29.) He charged them with the slaughter of the Redeemer, then stood before them without flinching. He chastised the sorcerer Simon, saying, "Thy money perish with thee." (Acts 8:20.) He stood before his brethren and announced a major policy change in the church whereby gentiles might be accepted.

Simon Peter was spiritual and prophetic. He received the revelations concerning the church. Angels accompanied him in and released him from the prison, and a great vision opened the door to millions of honest souls.

His testimony was as the rock, his faith unwavering. The Savior, abandoned by others, asked Peter, "Will ye also go away?" (John 6:67). Peter replied, "Lord, to whom shall we go? thou hast the words of eternal life" (John 6:68). Shortly before the crucifixion, the Lord asked, "But whom say ye that I am?" (Matthew 16:15). The answer revealed from God expressed the power and character of Peter: "Thou art the Christ, the Son of the living God" (Matthew 16:17). The Savior replied, "Flesh and blood hath not revealed it unto thee, but my Father which is in heaven" (Matthew 16:17). Heavenly messengers he had seen; martyrs he had accompanied; with the Son of God he had lived. The Comforter had come, and never was there faltering or questioning in his mind again.

Peter's Teachings

The teachings of Simon Peter are to all people, even to the latest generation. He bore testimony constantly of the divinity of the Christ. As he had been forgiven of his weaknesses, he now urged all men to forgive. He urged the chaste and virtuous life. He taught honesty and urged that members live in peace with the gentiles. This apostle taught his people to honor kings, governments, the laws; to endure grief, suffering, and buffeting patiently; and to consider revilement and suffering for the Lord's sake a blessing. Perhaps he had seen much marital unhappiness, for he commanded wives to be subject to and convert their unbelieving husbands through their own goodness and meekness. He commanded the husbands to honor their wives as partners, to love them, to be compassionate to them, and to treasure them. He urged parents to be kind to children and the posterity to honor and obey the parents. He urged employers to be honorable and just with their workers and employees to give service willingly. He urged the clean and constructive life and forbade company with rioters, winebibbers, revelers, banqueters, idolaters, and lustful ones. He urged service in the church, the sober life, a vigilant faith, and works leading toward perfection.

The great leader frequently repeated his testimony as an eyewitness and an ear witness to spectacular and eventful happenings. Foreshadowing the apostasy, he testified that false teachers with damnable heresies would come after his departing to deny the Lord and to make merchandise of the souls of men. (See 2 Peter 2:1-3.) He placed the divine stamp of approval on the writings of the Old Testament and unfolded the history of the world, which covered the flood, the destruction of Sodom and Gomorrah, and other important events. Again and again, he preached the law of chastity and cleanliness and denounced the evils of sporting, feasting, adultery, incontinence, and covetousness.

As he neared martyrdom, drinking a bitter cup somewhat like his Master and Teacher, he made sure that the world would know his witness and sureness. Sitting figuratively on the brink of his grave, he made a solemn declaration which has been read by countless millions. To the members of the church, he prayed that they might have a "knowledge of God, and of Jesus our Lord." (2 Peter 1:2.) He gloried in the "exceeding great and precious promises: that by these ye might be partakers of the divine nature, having escaped the corruption that is in the world through lust." (2 Peter 1:4.)

Peter continued:

> *Wherefore the rather, brethren, give diligence to make your calling and election sure...*
>
> *Yea, I think it meet, as long as I am in this tabernacle, to stir you up by putting you in remembrance;*
>
> *Knowing that shortly I must put off this my tabernacle, even as our Lord Jesus Christ hath shewed me.*
>
> *Moreover I will endeavor that ye may be able after my decease to have these things always in remembrance.*
>
> *For we have not followed cunningly devised gables, when we made known unto you the power and coming of our Lord Jesus Christ, but were eyewitnesses of his majesty.*
>
> *For he received from God the Father honour and glory, when there came such a voice to him from the excellent glory, This is my beloved Son, in whom I am well pleased.*
>
> *And this voice which came from heaven we heard, when we were with him in the holy mount.* (2 Peter 1:10, 13-18.)

When his work was done, his testimony borne, his witness delivered, and his numbered days run out, Satan who had long desired him was now permitted to take him in martyrdom. His testimony came from his dying lips.

But Simon Peter was not dead. Important changes came to him—the dissolution of his body, but also the resurrection of his soul. With his loyal associates, James and John, Simon Peter returned to earth, bridging the gap of darkened centuries. Together they appeared on the banks of the Susquehanna River in Pennsylvania, where Peter delivered to the young prophets the keys of the kingdom, which the apostles possessed from the Lord Jesus Christ.

The apostle lives. The weak things of the world confounded the wise. Millions have read his testimony. His powerful witness has stirred multitudes. Through the countless ages of eternity, he will live and extend his influence over the children of this earth. With his brethren, the Twelve, he will judge the nations.

My young brothers and sisters, I hope that you can love and accept the great prophet, Peter, as I feel in my heart to do. In the name of Jesus Christ. Amen.

Notes and Sources

Chapter One

1. Joseph Fielding Smith, comp. *Teachings of the Prophet Joseph Smith.* 1968 ed., p. 365.
2. Bruce R. McConkie. *Doctrinal New Testament Commentary, Volume 1: The Gospels.* Bookcraft, 1965, pp. 401-402. Used by permission.
3. James E. Talmage. *Jesus the Christ.* 1962 ed., p. 700-701. See also Acts 1: 13-16. See also the author's book, *Mary, Mother of Jesus,* Cedar Fort, 2001, p. 148.
4. James E. Talmage. *Jesus the Christ,* 1962 ed., p. 701.
5. Ibid., Note 2, p. 345.

Chapter Two

6. Alfred Edersheim. *The Life and Times of Jesus the Messiah.* Eighth Printing, Revised, 1896. Original printing was in 1883, in two volumes. Throughout this book, his work will be referred to as Edersheim. The quote is from Book 1, p. 227.
7. Ibid., p. 230.
8. Ibid., pp. 226-227.
9. Bruce R. McConkie. *The Mortal Messiah: From Bethlehem to Calvary.* Book 1 (Salt Lake City: Deseret Book, 1979), pp. 217-218. Used by permission.
10. *Sketches of Jewish Social Life in the Days of Christ.* 1876, p. 123.
11. Bruce R. McConkie. *The Mortal Messiah: From Bethlehem to Calvary.* Book 1 (Salt Lake City: Deseret Book, 1979), p. 218. Used by permission.
12. Ibid., p. 219. Used by permission.
13. Ibid., p. 219-220. Used by permission.

Chapter Three

14. Edersheim, Book 1, p. 228.
15. Ibid., p. 228.
16. Ibid., p. 228.
17. Ibid., p. 228.
18. The Torah is the complete body of Jewish religious law and learning.

19. Sages are recognized Jewish men of distinction and wisdom.
20. Edersheim, Book 1, p. 230.

Chapter Four

21. Edersheim, Book 1, pp. 230-231.
22. Ibid., p. 232.
23. Ibid., p. 232.
24. Bruce R. McConkie. *The Mortal Messiah: From Bethlehem to Calvary.* Book 1 (Salt Lake City: Deseret Book, 1979), pp. 42-43. Used by permission.

Chapter Five

25. Bruce R. McConkie. *The Mortal Messiah: From Bethlehem to Calvary.* Book 2, Deseret Book, 1980, pp. 105-106. Used by permission.
26. James E. Talmage. *Jesus the Christ.* 1962 ed., p. 221.

Chapter Six

27. Edersheim, Book 1, p. 473.
28. James E. Talmage. *Jesus the Christ.* 1962 ed., p. 218.
29. Ibid., p. 113.
30. The King James Version of the Bible published by The Church of Jesus Christ of Latter-day Saints. 1979, p. 621.
31. Edersheim, Book 1, p. 474.
32. James E. Talmage. *Jesus the Christ.* 1962 ed., p. 218.

Chapter Seven

33. James E. Talmage. *Jesus the Christ.* 1962 ed., pp. 219-220.
34. *See* the author's book, *Mary, Mother of Jesus.* Cedar Fort, 2001.
35. James E. Talmage. *Jesus the Christ.* 1962 ed., Note 1, p. 521.
36. Edersheim, Book 2, p. 602.
37. Bruce R. McConkie. *The Mortal Messiah: From Bethlehem to Calvary.* Book 4 (Salt Lake City: Deseret Book, 1981), p. 223. Used by permission.

Chapter Eight

38. Farrar, p. 76.
39. Ibid., p. 76.
40. Ibid., p. 77.

41. Ibid., p. 77.
42. Edersheim, Book 1, p. 346.
43. Ibid., p. 346.
44. Farrar, p. 77.
45. The King James Version of the Bible published by The Church of Jesus Christ of Latter-day Saints. 1979, p. 621.

Chapter Nine

46. Bruce R. McConkie. *A New Witness for the Articles of Faith*. Deseret Book, 1985, pp. 33-34. Used by permission.
47. Ibid., p. 35. Used by permission.
48. Ibid., pp. 38-39. Used by permission.
49. Ibid., pp. 38-39. Used by permission.
50. James E. Talmage. *Jesus the Christ*. 1962 ed., Note 1, p. 40.
51. Ibid., p. 140.
52. Edersheim, Book 1, p. 347.
53. Farrar, p. 78.
54. Bruce R. McConkie. *The Mortal Messiah: From Bethlehem to Calvary*. Book 1, (Salt Lake City: Deseret Book, 1979), p. 441. Used by permission.
55. Ibid., p. 441. Used by permission.
56. Farrar, p. 36.
57. Quoted in his work, *Sketches of Jewish Social Life in the Days of Christ*. p. 105, as printed in Bruce R. McConkie, *The Mortal Messiah: From Bethlehem to Calvary*. Book 1 (Salt Lake City: Deseret Book, 1979), p. 227. Used by permission.
58. Bruce R. McConkie. *The Mortal Messiah: From Bethlehem to Calvary*. Book 1 (Salt Lake City: Deseret Book, 1979), p. 223. Used by permission.
59. Ibid., Book 2, p. 32. Used by permission.
60. *See* the author's book, *Mysteries of the Kingdom*. Cedar Fort, 2000, p. 33.

Chapter Ten

61. James E. Talmage. *Jesus the Christ*. 1962 ed., p. 228.
62. Bruce R. McConkie. *The New Witness of the Articles of Faith*. Deseret Book, 1985, pp. 348-349. Used by permission.
63. Ibid., p. 349. Used by permission.
64. Ibid., p. 349. Used by permission.
65. Ibid., pp. 349-350. Used by permission.
66. Bruce R. McConkie. *Doctrinal New Testament Commentary,*

Volume 1, The Gospels. Bookcraft, 1965, p. 133. Used by permission.

67. Ibid., p. 133. Used by permission.
68. Bruce R. McConkie. *Mormon Doctrine.* 2nd ed, Bookcraft, 1966, p. 651. Used by permission.

Chapter Eleven

69. Edersheim, Book 1, p. 347.
70. Farrar, p. 81.
71. Edersheim, Book 1, pp. 347-348.
72. Ibid., Book 1, p. 348.
73. Farrar, p. 80.
74. James E. Talmage. *Jesus the Christ.* 1962 ed., p. 221.

Chapter Twelve

75. Regarding the marriage in Cana, the reader is referred to the author's book, *Mysteries of the Kingdom.* Cedar Fort, Inc., 2001, p. 33-41.
76. Farrar, p. 86.
77. James E. Talmage. *Jesus the Christ.* 1962 ed., p. 144.
78. Edersheim, Book 1, p. 356; Farrar, p. 86, Bruce R. McConkie, *The Mortal Messiah: From Bethlehem to Calvary.* Book 1, pp. 448-449.
79. Bruce R. McConkie. *Doctrinal New Testament Commentary, Volume 1, The Gospels.* Bookcraft, 1965, p. 437. Used by permission.

Chapter Thirteen

80. James E. Talmage. *Jesus the Christ.* 1962 ed., p. 153.
81. Farrar, p. 93.
82. Bruce R. McConkie. *The Mortal Messiah: From Bethlehem to Calvary.* Book 1 (Salt Lake City: Deseret Book, 1979), p. 455. Used by permission.
83. Ibid., p. 455. Used by permission.
84. James E. Talmage. *Jesus the Christ.* 1962 ed., pp. 159-160.
85. Ibid., p. 162.
86. Ibid., pp. 162-163.
87. Spencer W. Kimball. *Faith Precedes the Miracle.* Deseret Book, 1973, p. 43. Used by permission.
88. An address by President Heber J. Grant, Conference Report, April 4, 1941, p. 6. Used by permission from The Church of Jesus Christ of Latter-day Saints.

Chapter Fourteen

89. Bruce R. McConkie. *The Mortal Messiah: From Bethlehem to Calvary.* Deseret Book, Book 1, Deseret Book, 1979, p. 371. Used by permission.
90. Ibid., pp. 468-469. Used by permission.
91. James E. Talmage. *Jesus the Christ.* 1962 ed., p. 163.
92. Bruce R. McConkie. *The Mortal Messiah: From Bethlehem to Calvary.* Book 1, Deseret Book, 1979, p. 480. Used by permission.
93. James E. Talmage. *Jesus the Christ.* 1962 ed., pp. 163-164.
94. Farrar, p. 110.
95. James E. Talmage. *Jesus the Christ.* 1962 ed., pp. 164-165.
96. Bruce R. McConkie. *The Mortal Messiah: From Bethlehem to Calvary.* Book 1, Deseret Book, 1979, p. 482. Used by permission.
97. Bruce R. McConkie. *Doctrinal New Testament Commentary, The Gospels, Vol. 1.* Bookcraft, 1965, p. 148. Used by permission.
98. Bruce R. McConkie. *The Mortal Messiah: From Bethlehem to Calvary.* Deseret Book, Book 2, 1980, p. 32. Used by permission.
99. Edersheim, Book 1, p. 457.

Chapter Fifteen

100. James E. Talmage. *Jesus the Christ.* 1962 ed., pp. 165-166.
101. Edersheim, Book 1, p. 474.
102. Farrar, pp. 127-129.
103. Edersheim, Book 1, pp. 475-477, 485-486; James E. Talmage, *Jesus the Christ.* 1962 ed., pp. 183, 197-199; Bruce R. McConkie, *The Mortal Messiah: From Bethlehem to Calvary.* Book 2, Deseret Book, 1980, pp. 33-34.
104. Edersheim, Book 1, p. 476.
105. Farrar, p. 130.
106. James E. Talmage. *Jesus the Christ.* 1962 ed., p. 198.
107. Edersheim, Book 1, p. 476.
108. Farrar, p. 130.
109. Ibid., p. 131.

Chapter Sixteen

110. Edersheim, Book 1, p. 485.
111. Farrar, p. 127.
112. Edersheim, Book 1, p. 486.
113. Bruce R. McConkie. *The Mortal Messiah: From Bethlehem to Calvary.* Book 2, Deseret Book, 1980, p. 39. Used by permission.

114. Edersheim, Book 1, p. 501.
115. James E. Talmage. *Jesus the Christ.* 1962 ed., p. 190.
116. Ibid., p. 191.

Chapter Seventeen

117. Bruce R. McConkie. *The Mortal Messiah: From Bethlehem to Calvary.* Book 2, Deseret Book, 1980, pp. 99-100. Used by permission.
118. James E. Talmage. *Jesus the Christ.* 1962 ed., pp. 217-218.

Chapter Eighteen

119. James E. Talmage. *Jesus the Christ.* 1962 ed., p. 335.
120. Ibid., Note 6, p. 346.
121. Farrar, p. 218.
122. Ibid., p. 219.
123. Edersheim, Book 1, p. 693.
124. James E. Talmage. *Jesus the Christ.* 1962 ed., pp. 336-337.
125. Bruce R. McConkie. *The Mortal Messiah: From Bethlehem to Calvary.* Book 2, Deseret Book, 1980, pp. 286-287. Used by permission.
126. Farrar, p. 219.

Chapter Nineteen

James E. Talmage. *Jesus the Christ.* 1962 ed., p. 339.
Ibid., pp. 341-342.
Ibid., p. 343.
Ibid., p. 344.
Ibid., p. 344.

Chapter Twenty

132. Edersheim, Book 2, p. 36.
133. James E. Talmage. *Jesus the Christ.* 1962 ed., p. 349.
134. Farrar, pp. 234-235.
135. James E. Talmage. *Jesus the Christ.* 1962 ed., pp. 350-351.
136. Ibid., p. 353.

Chapter Twenty-One

137. James E. Talmage. *Jesus the Christ.* 1962 ed., p. 360.

Chapter Twenty-Two

138. James E. Talmage. *Jesus the Christ*. 1962 ed., p. 361.
139. Joseph Fielding Smith, comp. *Teachings of the Prophet Joseph Smith*, 1938, p. 274.
140. Bruce R. McConkie. *The Mortal Messiah: From Bethlehem to Calvary*. Book 3, Deseret Book, 1980, p. 39. Used by permission.
141. Bruce R. McConkie, *Doctrinal New Testament Commentary: The Gospel*. Vol. 1, pp. 389-390. Used by permission.
142. James E. Talmage. *Jesus the Christ*. 1962 ed., p. 362.
143. Lucille C. Tate. *Boyd K. Packer: A Watchman on the Tower*. Bookcraft, 1995, pp. 208-209. Used by permission.

Chapter Twenty-Three

144. Farrar, pp. 245-246.
145. Edersheim, Book 2, p. 86.
146. Farrar, p. 273.
147. Ibid., p. 274.
148. James E. Talmage. *Jesus the Christ*. 1962 ed., p. 364.

Chapter Twenty-Four

149. Bruce R. McConkie. *The Mortal Messiah: From Bethlehem to Calvary*. Book 3, Deseret Book, 1980, p. 54. Used by permission.
150. Edersheim, Book 2, p. 92.
151. James E. Talmage. *Jesus the Christ*. 1962 ed., Note 1, p. 376.
152. Edersheim, Book 2, pp. 94-95.
153. Farrar, p. 277.
154. Ibid., p. 277.
155. James E. Talmage. *Jesus the Christ*. 1962 ed. p. 370.
156. Farrar, p. 278.
157. Joseph Fielding Smith, comp. *Teachings of the Prophet Joseph Smith*, 1938, p. 158.
158. Bruce R. McConkie. *Mormon Doctrine*. 2nd ed., 1966, Bookcraft, p. 803. Used by permission.
159. Elder George Q. Cannon, An Address delivered Sunday evening, January, 12, 1873, as written in *Journal of Discourses*, Volume 15, p. 300.
160. James E. Talmage. *Jesus the Christ*. 1962 ed., p. 375.
161. Joseph Fielding Smith. *Doctrines of Salvation*. Vol. 2, Bookcraft, 1955, p. 165. Used by permission.
162. President Heber C. Kimball, An address delivered in the Tabernacle,

June 7, 1862, as recorded in the *Journal of Discourses*, Volume 9, p. 327.
163. James E. Talmage. *Jesus the Christ*. 1962 ed., p. 371.
164. Bruce R. McConkie. *Doctrinal New Testament Commentary: The Gospels*. Volume 1, Bookcraft, 1965, p. 403. Used by permission.
165. Bruce R. McConkie. *The Mortal Messiah: From Bethlehem to Calvary*. Book 3, Deseret Book, 1980, p. 63. Used by permission.

Chapter Twenty Five

166. Edersheim, Book 2, p. 101.
167. James E. Talmage. *Jesus the Christ*. 1962 ed., p. 378.
168. Ibid., pp. 378-379.
169. Farrar, p. 280.
170. James E. Talmage. *Jesus the Christ*. 1962 ed., p. 381.
171. Ibid., p. 382.
172. Farrar, p. 285.
173. James E. Talmage. *Jesus the Christ*. 1962 ed., p. 383.
174. Farrar, p. 286.
175. Ibid., p. 286.
176. Ibid., p. 286.
177. James E. Talmage. *Jesus the Christ*. 1962 ed., pp. 383-384.
178. Ibid., p. 384.

Chapter Twenty-Six

179. James E. Talmage. *Jesus the Christ*. 1962 ed., p. 386.
180. Ibid., pp. 387-388.
181. Ibid., p. 392.
182. Edersheim, Book 2, p. 117.

Chapter Twenty-Seven

183. James E. Talmage. *Jesus the Christ*. 1962 ed., pp. 478-479.
184. Bruce R. McConkie. *Doctrinal New Testament Commentary: The Gospels*. Volume 1, Bookcraft, 1965, p. 558. Used by permission.

Chapter Twenty-Eight

185. James E. Talmage. *Jesus the Christ*. 1962 ed., pp. 510-511.
186. Farrar, p. 375.
187. James E. Talmage. *Jesus the Christ*. 1962 ed., p. 524.

Chapter Twenty-Nine

188. Farrar, pp. 422-423.

189. James E. Talmage. *Jesus the Christ.* 1962 ed., p. 592.
190. Ibid., pp. 592-593.
191. Farrar, p. 424.
192. Edersheim, Book 2, p. 485.
193. Bruce R. McConkie. *The Mortal Messiah: From Bethlehem to Calvary.* Book 4, Deseret Book, p. 24. Used by permission.
194. Edersheim, Book 2, p. 488.

Chapter Thirty

195. James E. Talmage. *Jesus the Christ.* 1962 ed., pp. 593, 617.
196. Farrar, p. 425.
197. Edersheim, Book 2, pp. 492-495.
198. Ibid., Book 2, p. 498.
199. Bruce R. McConkie. *The Mortal Messiah: From Bethlehem to Calvary.* Book 4, Deseret Book, 1981, p. 37. Used by permission.
200. Ibid., Book 4, pp. 37-38. Used by permission.
201. James E. Talmage. *Jesus the Christ.* 1962 ed., p. 596.

Chapter Thirty-One

202. Edersheim, Book 2, p. 506.
203. James E. Talmage. *Jesus the Christ.* 1962 ed., p. 599.
204. Ibid., p. 600.

Chapter Thirty-Two

205. James E. Talmage. *Jesus the Christ.* 1962 ed., pp. 610-11, 620.

Chapter Thirty-Three

206. Bruce R. McConkie. *The Mortal Messiah: From Bethlehem to Calvary.* Book 4, Deseret Book, p. 125. Used by permission.
207. Ibid., p. 124. Used by permission.
208. James E. Talmage. *Jesus the Christ.* 1962 ed., p. 612.

Chapter Thirty-Four

209. Edersheim, Book 2, pp. 541-542.
210. James E. Talmage. *Jesus the Christ.* 1962 ed., p. 615.
211. Ibid., pp. 615-616.

Chapter Thirty-Five

212. James E. Talmage. *Jesus the Christ.* 1962 ed., p. 630.

213. Joseph F. Smith, Second Counselor in the First Presidency, from an address given January 20, 1895. As printed in *The Deseret Weekly*, February 16, 1895, p. 259.
214. James E. Talmage. *Jesus the Christ.* 1962 ed., pp. 678-679.
215. Ibid., p. 272. Used by permission.
216. James E. Talmage. *Jesus the Christ.* 1962 ed., p. 691.
217. Ibid., p. 693.
218. Ibid., p. 693.
219. President Brigham Young, An address delivered in the Tabernacle, at Salt Lake City, Utah, on Sunday, December 23, 1866, as recorded in *Journal of Discourses*, Volume 11, p. 274.
220. Elder George Q. Cannon, An address delivered in the Tabernacle, at Salt Lake City,Utah on August 15, 1869, as recorded in *Journal of Discourses*, Volume 14, p. 53.
221. President George A. Smith, First Counselor to President Brigham Young, An address delivered in the Tabernacle, at Salt Lake City, Utah, on August 13, 1971, as recorded in *Journal of Discourses*, Volume 14, p. 211.
223. James E. Talmage. *Jesus the Christ.* 1962 ed., p. 694.

Chapter Thirty-Six

Bruce R. McConkie. *The Millennial Messiah.* Deseret Book, 1982, pp. 118-119. Used by permission.
President Heber C. Kimball, First Counselor to President Brigham Young, An Address delivered in the Tabernacle, at Salt Lake City, Utah, on February 9, 1862, as recorded in the *Journal of Discourses*, Vol. 9, p. 376.

Index

McKay, 74, wrote a small booklet, *Wist Ye Not That I Must Be About My Father's Business*, 71; Elder McConkie uses time frame of, 71; a brief biography of, 78

Coasts of Caesarea Philippi, 121; explanation about 121

Cornelius, the vision of, 118; Peter met, 119; the gospel was introduced to, 118-119

Council of the Twelve Apostles, prophet and seers and revelators are members of the, 45-46

Crucifixion (Martyrdom) of Peter, Jesus told of the, 223-224; President Brigham Young's comments about the, 224; Elder George Q. Cannon's comments about the, 224; President George A. Smith's comments about the, 224

Deaf and dumb spirit, 153-154

Death of Jesus, the month and day and year of the, 217; events that transpired the third day following the, 217-220

Death of Peter, 228

Deliverer, the Jews looked forward for a, 14; Peter prayed for a, 14

Deny Jesus, Peter was told three times he would, 195; three times Peter did, 210-212

Dwelling Cloud, (Shekinah) the cloud which manifested the presence and glory of God, 146

Edersheim, Alfred, on difference between a Jewish and Gentile family, 5-6; a brief biography of, 7; fish was important in the diet of the Jews, 21; Zebedee and his sons were men of means, 23; Salome was the sister of Mary the mother of Jesus, 27; Salome was the wife of Zebedee, 27; Salome was the mother of John, 27; John was the cousin of Jesus, 27; time Andrew and John spent with Jesus, 31; Simon's designated name Peter, 35; the marital age of Jewish males, 38; about the first four disciples; 47; the disciples were followers not yet to be called apostles, 48; the disciples left Jesus in Galilee and returned to their homes, 78; Jesus called Peter, Andrew, James, and John to be permanent disciples, 79-80; Peter lowering his net as instructed by Jesus, 83; Peter's mother-in-law, 87; Peter's request to walk on the water, 105; that the dial pointed to the hour of Jesus' death, 115; the apostles perhaps thought the Christ was speak of his death in symbolic language, 132; about

83-84; the disciples permanently followed, 84-85; performed healings in or near Peter's home, 87-94; went to pray, 90; Peter and other disciples found, 90; the people wanted, to stay, 90; comments to the people and his disciples by, 90; heals a man with palsy, 92-93; prayed to know the Twelve, 98; the calling of the Twelve by, 95-100; the five thousand who were fed wanted to compel, to be their king, 102-103; constrained the apostles to enter a ship, 102-103; spent the night in prayer, 103; walked on the Sea of Galilee, 104-109; rescued Peter on the Sea of Galilee, 107; gently chided Peter, 107; entered the ship with Peter, 107; was the bread of life; 111; strong doctrine by, caused many to fall away, 111; asked the Twelve if they would go away, 112; told that one of the Twelve was a devil, who was Judas Iscariot, 113; about the law of cleanliness, 116-118; Peter counsels, 131-133; rebuked Peter, 133; told Judas Iscariot was the betrayer, 188; told Judas to do his betrayal quickly, 188; washing of the apostle's feet, 184-186; the sacramental ordinance, 188-192; told Peter he would deny, three times, 195; his agonizing atonement in Gethsemane; 194-202; betrayed by a kiss by Judas Iscariot, 204; allowed his arrest, 204-205; healed the severed ear of Malchus, 205-206; taken to various rulers, 209; the denials of Peter regarding, 210-213; Peter present at the death of, 216; the month and day and year of the death of, 217; events that transpired three days after the death of, 217-220

Jew, Peter was a, 3

Jewish children, formal instruction and schooling of, 13

Jewish family, Peter was born in a, 3, 5, 7; explanation of a, 5-7; educational process of a, 9, 15-16

Jewish fathers, teaching of, 10-11

Jewish males, duty requirements of, 38; marital ages of, 38-39

Jewish mothers, teaching of, 9-10

Jewish women, marital ages of a, 39

Jews, the apostles are to build up the Church and regulate all the affairs secondly unto the, 44

John the apostle, statement made by our Lord, shall not taste of death, 134-135; our Lord's statement to Peter about the translation of, 224-225; the account of the translation of, 225

John the Baptist, Jesus was baptized by, 29; statement about Jesus by, 30; Andrew and John were disciples of, 30; ministered in Judea, 72; baptizing in Aenon near Salim because there was much water there, 73; disciples of, were concerned that Jesus was baptizing converts, 74; the answer to the disciples of, 74-75; the fate of, 75; appeared upon the Mount of Transfiguration, 143; appeared in 1829 to the Prophet Joseph Smith and Oliver Cowdery and conferred upon them the Aaronic Priesthood, 229-230; acted under the direction of Peter and James and John, 229

Jona (Jonas), Peter's and Andrew's father was, 17, 23

Jude, one of the Lord's half brother was, 58, 66

Judea, Jesus and Peter and other disciples ministered in, 72-73; John the Baptist ministered in, 73

Keys of the kingdom, Peter and James and John held the, 1; the Presidency of the High Priesthood holds the, 1; the Lord told Peter he would give him the, 126-127; Peter held all of the, 129; Peter and James and John received the, upon the Mount of Transfiguration, 138; Peter and James and John conferred upon the Prophet Joseph Smith and Oliver Cowdery the, 230-231

Kimball, Elder Spencer W. Kimball, explained that by inspiration President Heber J. Grant called Elder Ballard to be an apostle, 67

Kimball, President Heber C, stated that Peter was in the Kirtland Temple, 231-232

Kimball, President Spencer W. Kimball, an experience of Elder Boyd K. Packer with, 128-129; Peter, My Brother written by, 233-247

Kingdom of heaven, the Church of Jesus Christ is the, 126

Kirtland Temple, President Heber C. Kimball stated that Peter was in the, 231-231

Last supper, See Passover feast

Maintenance, women have claim on their husbands for, 40; children have claim on their parents for, 40; children have claim upon the Church for, 40

Malchus, Peter cut off the right ear of, 132; 205-206; Jesus healed the injury of, 206

Marriage in Cana, there was a, 55; Mary the mother of Jesus was at the, 55-56; Jesus along with Peter and Andrew and James and John and Philip and Nathanel were called to be at the, 55;

scholars believe that one of Mary's children was being married at the, 55; wedding festivity could have lasted a week at the, 55; Mary's request of Jesus to miraculously provide wine at the, 55-56; the disciples of Jesus believed on him at the, 57

Married, Peter and Andrew and James and John were, 37-40

Mary, the mother of Jesus was, 25-26; Salome was the sister of, 26-27; at the crucifixion of Jesus was, 26; scholars believe that one of the children of, was being married, 55; the request of Jesus to turn water into wine was made by, 55-56; Jesus' response to his mother, 56

Mary Magdalene, at the crucifixion of Jesus was, 26; at the tomb of Jesus was, 217-218; Peter and John were told of the empty tomb of Jesus by, 218

McConkie, Elder Bruce R, Peter and James and John were the First Presidency in their day, 1; Peter and James and John held the keys of the kingdom, 1; a brief biography of, 2; on difference between a Jewish and Gentile family, 6-7; the Deliverer, 14; wrote a brief description of Simon Peter, 17-18; Salome was the sister of Mary, 27; Salome was the wife of Zebedee, 27; Salome was the mother of James and John, 27; James and John were cousins of Jesus, 27; believing blood, 33-34; explanation about premortality, 33; the noble and great ones are sent to favored families, 33; Simon's designated name Peter, 35; Peter was known as the Rock and the Seer, 36; Peter and Andrew and James and John were forsaking all to follow Jesus, 37-38; the disciples were married and had families, 37-38; marital ages of Jewish men and women, 39; about apostles in the Church, 44; the President of the Church is the senior apostle, 44; the President of the Church is the presiding prophet, 45; the Lord told Peter that the gates of hell shall never prevail against the rock of revelation or seership, 46; about a revelator and revelators, 46; the brethren of Jesus were his half-brothers, 58-59; Jude wrote the epistle of Jude and James the Lord's brother was to administer in the apostleship, 59, 66; the time frame of our Lord's formal ministry, 71; Jesus and Peter and other disciples preached in Judea, 72; Jesus conferred the priesthood upon Peter and his fellow disciples, 76; Jesus personally performed water baptisms, 77; Jesus performed all other ordinances essential to salvation and exaltation, 77; the disciples witnessed many things Jesus did, 77-78; Jesus was going to

Passover Feast, the Paschal feast is the same as the, 52; about the, 52; Farrar's statement about our Lord's last, 52-53; during the formal ministry of Jesus there were four, 72; Peter and John prepared the, 177-179; food eaten at the, 181; seating order of Jesus and the apostles at the, 182-183; Judas was told he was the betrayer at the, 183, 185-188; ordinance of washing of feet introduced at the, 184-185; sacramental ordinance introduced at the, 188-189; conversation between Peter and Jesus at the, 192

Perea, 166

Permanent disciples, Jesus called Peter and Andrew and James and John to be, 80-81; the disciples became, 85

Peter, a noble and great spirit was, 2; the senior apostle was, 2; the person who conducted the meeting to chose a new apostle was, 2; educational process of, 9-22; a brief description of, 17-18; the brother of Andrew was, 17; Andrew's fishing partner was, 21; James and John were fishing partners with, 21-22; well-to-do financially, 23; Andrew told, he had found the Messiah, 32; a special witness of the name of Christ was, 45; President of the Church was, 45-46; presiding prophet was, 45; the seer for the Church was, 46; the prophet and seer and revelator for the whole Church was, 46; in attendance at the Marriage of Cana was, 55; Judean ministry of, 73; the baptism of, 76; priesthood conferred upon, 76; Jesus told, to let down his nets for a draught, 82; the response to Jesus by, 82; submissive and obedient was, 82; Edersheim's statement about, 83; depart from me spoken by, 83; was astonished at the number of fish caught, 84; Jesus told, he would henceforth catch me, 84; brought his ship to shore and followed Jesus, 84; events in or near the home of, 87-94; by the temple, healed a lame man from birth, 89-90; about the preparation of, 93; spoke boldly to the rulers in Jerusalem, 93-94; called to be the senior apostle, 98-100; walked on the Sea of Galilee, 104-108; was a man of action, a man of God, and a man of faith, 108; confession of belief, 112-113; observed Jesus healing people in Gennesaret, 109-110; when President of the Church people were healed by the shadow of, passing by, 110; confession of belief that Jesus had the words of eternal life, 112; told that one of the Twelve was a devil, 113; the law of cleanliness and, 115-118; purging all men and, 118; Cornelius and, 118-119; another confession by, 121-123; the Lord told, he would give him the

Premortality, lived for a long time in, 33; the ability to believe based on, 33

President of the Church, the senior apostle is the, 44; Peter was the, 44; presiding prophet on earth is the, 45

Priesthood, Jesus conferred upon Peter and his fellow disciples the, 76

Prophet, the President of the Church is the presiding, 45

Prophets, persons who have the testimony of Jesus are, 45; the First Presidency and the Twelve Apostles are sustained as, 45

Psalms, the earliest hymns were the, 11

Pulpit, Jesus preached from a floating, 82

Purifying, apostate Jewish beliefs about, 74

Purse or scrip, explanation of, 194; our Lord revoked the decree to go without, 194

Resurrection, the disciples were present when Jesus taught his own, 63-66; Elijah and Moses spoke of Jesus' death and, 141; the apostles were told by Jesus of his death and, 155

Revelation, Peter was told that the gates of hell would never prevail against the rock of, 46; statement by the Prophet Joseph Smith that the Church was built upon the rock of, 125-126

Revelator, anyone who receives revelation from the Lord is a, 46

Revelators, President of the Church and members of the First Presidency and Council of the Twelve Apostles are called, 46

Rock and the Seer, Peter was known as the, 36, 40; the Church not built upon Peter the, 125-126

Sabbath meals, festive occasions were, 87-88

Sacramental ordinance, our Lord introduced the, 188-189; to be administered at Adam-ondi-Ahman, 189-191;

Salome, the sister of Mary was, 26-27; the wife of Zebedee was, 27; the mother of James and John was, 27

Sea of Galilee, description of, 79-80; Jesus and Peter walked on the, 103-108

Seer, Peter was known as the Rock and the, 36, 40

Seers, specially selected prophets are called, 45-46; specially selected, are authorized to use the Urim and Thummim, 45-46